D1488267

DATE•ONOMICS

How Dating Became a
Lopsided Numbers Game

JON BIRGER

WORKMAN PUBLISHING
NEW YORK

Central Islip Public Library
33 Hawthorne Avenue
Central Islip, NY 11722

3 1800 00314 8562

Copyright © 2015 by Jon Birger

All rights reserved. No portion of this book may be reproduced—mechanically, electronically, or by any other means, including photocopying—without written permission of the publisher. Published simultaneously in Canada by Thomas Allen & Son Limited.

Excerpt on page 35 is from *The New York Times*, February 5, 2010 © 2010 The New York Times. All rights reserved. Used by permission and protected by the copyright laws of the United States. The printing, copying, redistribution, or retransmission of this content without express written permission is prohibited.

Library of Congress Cataloging-in-Publication Data is available.

ISBN 978-0-7611-8717-2 (hardcover)
ISBN 978-0-7611-8208-5 (paperback)

Design by Becky Terhune

Workman books are available at special discounts when purchased in bulk for premiums and sales promotions as well as for fund-raising or educational use. Special editions or book excerpts also can be created to specification. For details, contact the Special Sales Director at the address below, or send an email to specialmarkets@workman.com.

Workman Publishing Co., Inc.
225 Varick Street
New York, NY 10014-4381
workman.com

WORKMAN is a registered trademark of Workman Publishing Co., Inc.

Printed in the United States

First printing July 2015

10 9 8 7 6 5 4 3 2 1

CONTENTS

Chapter 1
The Man Deficit

··

My friend Sarah Donovan* is a gem. She's kind. She's funny. She's an Ivy Leaguer, and a head-turner too. Professionally, Sarah is a star: a top journalist as well as a familiar face and voice on television and radio.

Sarah is also 41 years old and unmarried. And it is this predicament—one that saddens Sarah, perplexes her friends, and frustrates her parents—that is the catalyst for this book. American cities are filled with Sarah Donovans—educated, successful, personable, often attractive women whose dating woes make little sense to those around them. Their stories are well chronicled in novels, movies, and TV shows, from *Bridget Jones's Diary* to *Sex and the City* to *Girls*. On-screen, these tales usually have happy endings. In real life? It's not so easy. "Come to think of it, I don't think I've ever had someone

*Sarah Donovan is a pseudonym, as are other names denoted with an asterisk. Some biographical details have been altered to hide their identities.

ask me if they knew any nice girls for their son," said Jeffrey Sirkman, the longtime rabbi at Larchmont Temple in Larchmont, New York, and a keen observer of the marriage market. "But just about every week some mother or father will ask me whether I know of any nice guys for their daughter. Why is that?"

Why indeed. Why is it that women like Donovan struggle to find marriage-material men even as male counterparts with less going for them seem to have little trouble with the opposite sex? Attempts to answer such questions have spawned a cottage industry of self-help books for women—dating guides that portray the failure to find Mr. Right as a strategic problem, one that can be fixed by playing hard to get or by following a few simple dating "rules." Underlying all such advice is an assumption that the perceived shortage of college-educated men—a phenomenon that I call "the man deficit"—is actually a mirage. At birth there are *more* boys than girls: 1.05 boys are born in the U.S. for every 1 girl. So if college-educated women just become better daters—if they can get inside men's heads and understand what makes them commit—there should be enough college-educated men out there for everyone.

But what if the problem is not strategic? What if most of the good men are taken? What if a disproportionate number of the single guys still out there really are incorrigible commitment-phobes just looking for a good time? What if it doesn't just *seem* as if there's a third more single women than men in every semi-upscale bar in Manhattan or Dallas or L.A.? What if the demographics actually bear that out? What if the hookup culture on today's college campuses and the wild ways of the big-city singles scene have little to do with changing values and a whole lot to do with lopsided gender ratios that pressure 19-year-old girls to put out and discourage 30-year-old guys from settling down?

What if, in other words, the man deficit were real?

Well, it is real, and the numbers are so shocking it's a wonder they are not talked about incessantly. According to 2012 population estimates from the U.S. Census Bureau's American Community Survey, there are 5.5 million college-educated women in the U.S. between the ages of 22 and 29 versus 4.1 million such men. In other words, the dating pool for college graduates in their twenties really does have 33 percent more women than men—or four women for every three men. Among college grads age 30 to 39, there are 7.4 million women versus 6.0 million men, which is five women for every four men. These lopsided gender ratios may add up to sexual nirvana for heterosexual men, but for heterosexual women—especially those who put a high priority on getting married and having children in wedlock—they represent a demographic time bomb.

How exactly did gender ratios for the college educated get so skewed? The simple answer is that women have been attending college at higher rates than men since the 1980s, and at a *much* higher rate since the late 1990s. In 2012, 34 percent more women than men graduated from four-year colleges, and this gaping gender gap in college education spilled over into the post-college dating pool long ago. The shortage of college-educated men—a 1.4 million–man deficit among those 22 to 29—has been exacerbated by the increased reluctance of college-educated Americans to marry those lacking a college degree. According to separate research published by University of Pennsylvania economist Jeremy Greenwood and by UCLA sociologists Christine Schwartz and Robert Mare, educational intermarriage is less common today than at any point over the past half century.

As poor as the marriage market may be for educated, 40-something women like my friend Sarah, the long-term outlook for young millennial women is decidedly worse. In the U.S. there are 39 percent more college-grad women age 24 and younger than there are men in the same age cohort, according to Census data. (The man deficit is larger post-college than during college in part because foreign students are disproportionately male.) In Manhattan, the pool of 24-and-under college grads has 38 percent more women than men. In Raleigh, North Carolina, the gap is 49 percent. In Miami and Washington, D.C., it's 86 percent and 49 percent, respectively. Los Angeles: 37 percent. Moreover, for reasons I'll explore later involving the demographics of the gay and lesbian community, the Census numbers probably *understate* the true size of heterosexual gender gaps in LGBTQ-friendly cities such as Miami, New York, and L.A. The bottom line is that by the time today's educated, early-twenties women are ready to marry, they'll be confronted with a marriage market far more daunting than the one their older cousins or younger aunts graduated into twenty years ago. Meanwhile, young male college grads now enjoy such an overabundance of sexual options that it will be interesting to see when (or if?) some of these men choose to settle down.

This book will make the case that the college and post-college hookup culture, the decline in marriage rates among college-educated women, and the dearth of marriage-material men willing to commit are all by-products of lopsided gender ratios and a massive undersupply of college-educated men. The conventional explanations for these trends all seem rooted in a kind of social entropy in which male-female relations naturally devolve from the traditional to the libertine. Despite a wealth of academic research showing how sex ratios affect dating behavior, demographics never seem to be part of the conversation.

Consider a 1,900-word *New York Times* article from January 2013 on the city's hookup culture. The *Times* story—headline: "The End of Courtship?"—documented the demise of traditional first dates as well as the rise of debauched one-night stands and the pseudo-relationships that follow. "Hey babe, what are you up to this weekend?" was the Thursday night text message one guy would send his off-and-on sex partner. The *Times* story blamed the hookup culture on everything from technology ("Online research makes the first date feel unnecessary") to the lousy economy ("Faced with a lingering recession, a stagnant job market, and mountains of student debt, many young people—particularly victims of the 'mancession'—simply cannot afford to invest a fancy dinner or show in someone they may or may not click with").

Not once did the *Times* mention gender ratios or the fact that New York City has 100,000 more women than men who are college educated and under age 35. In New York, with a new crop of college grads arriving every summer, the city's dating pool "is like a market that just won't clear," said Andrew Beveridge, a demographer and sociology professor at New York's Queens College. Consider Murray Hill, which has become a hot neighborhood for young Manhattan singles. According to Census tract data, in the age 20 to 29 cohort, there are 2.3 never-married women in Murray Hill for every 1 never-married man. In the trendy, club-filled Meatpacking District, there are 2.2 never-married women for every 1 never-married man. With numbers like these, it's no wonder that men feel no rush to marry and that women stop playing hard to get.

There is a popular misconception that the oversupply of college-educated women is a phenomenon unique to New York and a handful of other major cities. Melanie Notkin—an author and entrepreneur whom I happen to know a little and like a lot—made this argument in her terrific memoir, *Otherhood*, an exploration of the meaning of being single and childless in contemporary America. "There are lots of women, including ambitious women who move to New York City to work, expecting to meet ambitious men," Notkin wrote. "Only, the men don't follow."

New York City is a bad dating market for college-educated women. The Census numbers actually understate the true size of the city's gender gap. Moreover, I'm not surprised that Notkin perceives ambitious men to be in particularly short supply. As we'll see later, lopsided gender ratios can impact people's drive, ambition, and even their earnings. However, what Notkin experiences daily in New York is not a problem unique to New York. Tammie Collins, founder of the Cleveland dating agency True Match Mixers, told me her dating pool has three college-educated women for every one college-educated man. "The women are all off the charts," said Collins, whose agency offers speed dating as well as traditional matchmaking. "I spend a lot of time coaching the women, trying to get them to lower their standards."

Suzanna Mathews, a professional matchmaker in Wichita, Kansas, had a similar story. Before Mathews and I spoke, she actually posted on Facebook to get clients' reactions to the notion that single women in New York have it worse than they do. One woman's reply: "I think New York or California women would be shocked at the men available in our area if they think it's bad where they are!" It is so bad, said Mathews, that some educated women just give up: "I'm hearing more and more single women say they'd rather stay single than put up with men's shenanigans. They don't want to play men's games—dress like a video ho or be at their beck and call."

While the dating math for educated women is somewhat more challenging in the eastern U.S. than out West, Census data shows there is no gender ratio divide when it comes to rural versus urban or small town versus big city. Rural states such as Arkansas, Mississippi, Montana, Oklahoma, and West Virginia all have man deficits much larger than those found in urban states such as California, New Jersey, and New York. Indeed, Mississippi and Montana have 54 percent and 52 percent more college-educated women than men age 22 to 29 as compared to 20 percent and 30 percent more such women than men in California and New York.

Other explanations for changes in the national dating market tend to conflate cause and effect. According to Census data, the number of age 30-to-34, college-educated women who have never been married rose from 865,083 in 2007 to 1,133,956 in 2012—a 31 percent increase. Why? Hanna Rosin, author of *The End of Men*, has argued that this is largely by choice—that the modern woman no longer needs a traditional husband. More focused on careers and less interested in traditional relationships, today's young women now "behave in sexually aggressive ways that would have been unimaginable 20 years ago," Rosin wrote.

On that last point, Rosin and I agree. Hailee Katz,* a 25-year-old college grad in Manhattan whom I interviewed about millennial dating customs, seemed perplexed by my suggestion that some older women feel degraded by one particularly messy sex act. "Hmm, I'd say coming anywhere is pretty game," Katz told me. "It doesn't happen all the time. And guys still ask permission—or at least give you the 'head's up.' But rather honestly, if this is someone you are going down on frequently, then what is the real difference?"

Back to the original question, did women's attitudes toward sex and marriage really change *that* much between 2007 and 2012? Or could there be a simpler, demographic explanation for the declining marriage rates and for why more women are opting to put careers first, marry later, and adopt a more adventurous and less romantic approach toward sex and dating?

Consider that the career woman who turned 34 years old in 2007 started college in a year, 1991, when there were only 10 percent more women than men on college campuses. In contrast, a woman who turned 34 in 2012 likely started college in 1996, by which time the college gender gap had doubled to 20 percent. This explains why among college grads age 30 to 34, the number of never-married women increased 31 percent between 2007 and 2012, even as the number of never-married men increased only 22 percent. In the vernacular of the bestselling dating manuals, it's not that He's Just Not That Into You. It's that There Aren't Enough of Him.

Others blame cultural influences for chipping away at monogamy. Television, movies, and music all promote a freewheeling sexuality and general ambivalence toward marriage—or so the theory goes. Michael Medved, the conservative movie critic, summed it up this way: "Most of us live in a much better world than the one depicted by the media. And while you are trying to lead a decent, restrained life, TV promulgates the notion that everybody else is having a wild, debauched time and that you may be missing out. That is the true power of mass media—the power to redefine normal."

There's no question that pop culture exerts some influence over behavior. Everyone knows that kids routinely mimic the styles and mannerisms of their favorite athletes and pop stars. My quarrel with the pop-culture explanation is based purely on data. Everyone from neuroscientists to parents understands that adolescents are more susceptible to outside influence than mature adults. So if pop culture truly were influencing sexual behavior, teenagers should be having more sex than ever these days. In fact, U.S. teens are having significantly *less* sex today than teens did 30 years ago, at the height of the AIDS crisis. According to the U.S. Centers for Disease Control and Prevention, the percentage of girls age 15 to 19 who have had sexual intercourse fell from 51 percent to 43 percent between 1988 and 2010; among boys, the decline was 60 percent to 42 percent. So if Hollywood really is trying to promote promiscuity, it's doing a terrible job.

There is one demographic subset for which teenage sexual activity has not declined, and that subset is African Americans. In her 2013 book *Dollars and Sex*, economist Marina Adshade, a professor at the University of British Columbia, attributed the African American anomaly to simple supply and demand. "When we consider the observation that the recent high school completion rates for black men are between 7 and 12 percentage points lower than for black women," Adshade wrote, "all the evidence suggests that black teenage women are competing with each other and with women of other races for far fewer black men on the high school market."

I realize that most people do not want to think about supply and demand when contemplating matters of the heart. The idea that gender ratios influence whom we date, love, and have sex with is disconcerting. So too is the notion that college admissions offices are unwittingly pushing some women into promiscuity and dooming others to spinsterhood. I ran this by my single, 20-something friend Julia Bolton*—a Georgetown University grad—and got the following reaction: "Meh, 56:44 [the current female-to-male gender ratio for undergrads at Georgetown] doesn't seem like a statistically significant difference between gender so as to single-handedly account for why there's a rise in the hookup culture." When I pointed out to Julia that 56:44 means 27 percent more women than men—or five women for every four men—she got annoyed: "This is true, but do you really buy that? I absolutely don't buy this idea that women are putting out because there are more of them and if they don't put out, they'll get passed over for mating. That's just reductionist."

Expressed like *that*, it does sound a little reductionist. I am not implying that gender ratios are the only variable when it comes to whom we date or marry. My argument is more macro than micro—that gender ratios are the key variable in explaining long-term trends such as the decline in marriage rates and loosening sexual mores for heterosexual, college-educated men and women. The influence that gender ratios exert over behavior comes into sharper focus when comparing cities like New York and colleges like University of Georgia—dating markets that have oversupplies of women—to dissimilar dating markets with oversupplies of men.

In February 2010, *The New York Times* published an article examining how college life has been affected by rising female enrollments. One of the article's more revealing anecdotes came from Katie Deray, a University of Georgia senior who enrolled there from a Christian high school in Savannah. According to U.S. Department of Education data compiled by StudentAdvisor.com, the University of Georgia has a 62:38 female-to-male gender ratio, which means there are five female undergrads for every three male ones. This undersupply of men—or oversupply of women, depending on your perspective— was a source of great frustration for Deray. "If a guy is not getting what he wants, he can quickly and abruptly go to the next one, because there are so many of us," she complained. Deray said it was commonplace to see six provocatively clad women hovering around one or two guys at a party. Since this wasn't her style, Deray had yet to have a serious boyfriend in college.

What made Deray's story tough to read was where she

said she planned on moving after graduation. Deray said she hoped her dating odds would improve once she relocated to New York City for a job in the fashion industry. What Deray obviously did not realize was that New York City's demographics are no better for single women than the University of Georgia dating market she would be leaving behind. And since physical proximity and career choice influence the composition of one's dating pool—a topic I will explore later—Deray's decision to work in New York's fashion trade made it even less likely she would meet significant numbers of straight, single, dateable men after college.

Indeed, the photo that accompanied that *Times* story—six University of North Carolina women in a bar surrounding a guy in a trucker hat—is a scenario all too familiar to Manhattan women. Whether it's house parties, bars, dinner parties, or social events in the Hamptons, it's understood that most such gatherings will include a handful (or more) of attractive, well-dressed, successful women and only one or two eligible men. The situation becomes even more fraught for women in their late thirties and forties whose biological clocks are ticking. Donovan told me that women at such gatherings often try to get to eligible men they want to meet early on, lest someone else get to them first and make a connection. On the rare instance when a new single guy enters the room, Donovan described an "almost palpable, heightened state of awareness" among the women. They know—even if they are loath to admit it—"that a competition has just begun," because good single guys are so hard to come by. Even in casual settings—hanging out at the beach, running into someone at Bloomingdale's, or walking around downtown Manhattan on the weekend—when a single woman in her thirties gets introduced to, bumps into, or otherwise encounters a new, normal-looking, even slightly well-dressed single guy, "it is an event," Donovan said.

Some men, especially those who remain single into their late twenties and beyond, recognize the favorable market conditions and turn them to their advantage. "The goal for guys is to get as much ass as possible and then boast about it," said Jim Leveque,* a 31-year-old former college and minor league baseball player who now runs a personal training business in New York City. A good-looking guy with an engaging personality, Leveque's bar-crawling days are behind him: He is now happily married. But back in his single days, the women Leveque met at bars in Chelsea or the Meatpacking District would routinely text him nude or partially nude selfies—completely unsolicited—within hours of their encounters. "My friends and I would compare photos," he admitted somewhat sheepishly.

Whenever Leveque wanted to get together with a girl, he'd scroll through his photo library and decide which one to call. Given what was already on his iPhone, Leveque wasn't terribly worried about a girl saying no. And replenishing his call list was easy. If Leveque walked into a bar with a couple of buddies—and his friends are not ex-jocks, for whatever it's worth—it would not be long before five or six women descended on their table. "It's crazy," he told me. "I've dated all over the country—you know, the life of a minor league ballplayer—and I can tell you that the best place for guys by far is New York. My god, it's not even close."

The man deficit does not turn every guy into a lothario. Obviously there are still plenty of marriage-minded men. And some of them are nice, normal guys who simply cannot believe their luck. A friend of a friend is one such type—a kind, sweet, but not terribly attractive business executive from Oklahoma who now lives in New York. He was always dating attractive blonds—one a model—and he ultimately married a gorgeous event planner. "This city is unbelievable for guys like me," he said. "I tell all my guy friends they should move to New York."

Now compare the New York City dating market to that of Santa Clara County, California, home to Silicon Valley and the locale with the highest male-to-female ratio for under-30 college grads of any well-populated area in the United States. It is a common refrain among Valley types that there are not enough women; it's talked about almost as much as the shortage of engineers. San Jose, the county seat, is jokingly referred to as "Man Jose" by the locals, and with good reason: In the 22 to 29 age cohort, Santa Clara County has 37,410 never-married, college-grad men versus 27,147 never-married, college-grad women. That's 38 percent more men than women—essentially New York City in reverse. If the Manhattan dating scene is *Girls*, Santa Clara County could be *The Big Bang Theory.*

So how does the high ratio of educated men to women affect dating and marriage in Silicon Valley? Well, according to 2012 Census estimates, the marriage rate for college-educated women in Santa Clara County is abnormally high: 33 percent of the women age 22 to 29 are married, versus 31 percent nationally and 13 percent in Manhattan. Silicon Valley's marriages are more stable too: Only 4 percent of Santa Clara County women age 30 to 39 are separated or divorced, versus 7 percent nationally and in Manhattan.

Male competition for women is so fervent in Silicon Valley that some single women cannot believe their luck. "I think it's pretty good for the girls," Elizabeth Harris, a transplant from Los Angeles, told *The San Jose Mercury News* in 2009. (At the time of the interview, she was the only woman sitting at the bar at San Jose's Mission Ale House—aka the "Mission Male House.") "You can be more picky," Harris said. "They have to try harder. They all try to one-up each other."

Of course, single guys are less enamored with Silicon Valley's male-heavy gender ratio. "It's the attitude girls have because they can be picky, so they can blow off any dude they want," complained Rigo Pantoja, a 25-year-old bartender. "I think guys have to throw money at girls now to get more attention."

This book will use economics, sociology, and demographics to explain social trends and phenomena people feel to be true but cannot explain. Think of every grandmother who has shaken her head and announced—exasperated—that she cannot understand why her granddaughter does not have a nice man in her life. Think of the aunt at the wedding reception who wonders aloud why there's a table full of young, single women, yet no single men to sit them with. Think of the 30-something single career women in New York, Toronto, or Los Angeles who gather at brunch on Sundays and complain over mimosas that "There are no guys in this town." For these people, this book will finally deliver the tangible proof that will make them smack their hands down on their tables and say, "Aha! See? I KNEW it!"

Happily married for twenty years and a business journalist by trade, I stumbled onto this topic. The staffs at *Money* and *Fortune*, my last two employers, were both majority women, and I could never understand why so many of my favorite female colleagues seemed to have such trouble when it came to dating. By the time my wife and I turned 40, we both had a plethora of single female friends, yet no single men we could set them up with. We weren't alone. "Oh my goodness, my wife and I talk about that all the time!" said one former colleague when I informed him of the subject of my book. "Does the data back this up? Are there really more single women than men?"

My hope is that the statistical revelations in this book will be of comfort to educated women who may blame themselves for the failure to find Mr. Right. My fear, however, is that the reaction from at least some of these women will be more "screw you" than "thank you." They'll interpret the data as some sort of backdoor argument that today's young career women cannot have it all—that they cannot have a budding career or a fun sex life without jeopardizing future hope of marital bliss.

That is neither my argument nor my intent. For the record, I do not believe that marriage or even monogamy has to be the right choice for everyone. I do not care whether people prioritize career over family or vice versa. And I certainly don't care how much sex or how many partners consenting adults choose to have. Yes, my statistical analysis does indicate that college-educated women who wait till their thirties to get serious about dating are putting themselves into a more challenging marriage market. But that is not to say that educated women should never delay marriage. Everyone's priorities and aspirations are different. My goal is simply to make sure people's choices are informed ones.

This is not an advice book per se. But I do believe that enlightening women and men alike about how education, career, and geography can affect one's dating and marriage prospects can help everybody make better, more informed life decisions. Based on the more woman-friendly gender ratios in California, Colorado, and Washington State, for instance, "Go West, Young Woman" could be the new mantra for freshly minted college grads. But data also show that college-grad women do not have to change their zip codes to expand their dating pool. An undersupply of men among the college educated means there is an over-supply of men among the non-college educated. Given this demographic reality, I believe that a rise in what I call mixed-collar marriages—i.e., pairings of white-collar women and blue-collar men—is inevitable.

Long term, the only way to fix the man deficit is by increasing the number of boys attending college. How to accomplish this is a topic I explore in the final chapter. One of my many goals for this book is to spark a fierce and long overdue debate about whether the increasingly lopsided gender ratios at most colleges are bad not only for the young men forgoing college but for female under-grads as well.

The title of the next chapter, "How We Got to 57:43," refers to the current gender ratio among U.S. college students. Of course, explaining how we got to 57:43 is sort of pointless if readers do not understand what 57:43 actually means. So before proceeding, I'm going to give a quick primer on the statistics and calculations I use to make various arguments in this book. None of the math is terribly complicated, so if you're already comfortable with math and with statistics, feel free to skip ahead.

I'm a business writer in my day job, which means that A) I have to be good with numbers and B) I'm usually writing for people who are number savvy them-selves. But writing a book about dating for a mainstream audience is quite different from writing about corporate earnings for the readers of *Fortune* magazine. I did not appreciate how different until someone who read an early draft admitted he did not realize that a 60:40 ratio of women to men was that big a gender gap. Well, it is big: 60:40 means a population with 50 percent more women than men.

In general, I believe "how much more" questions are best answered with percentages. Percentages put quantitative differences into proper context. Let's say I'm writing about oil (something I do a lot), and an editor asks me how much more crude oil Saudi Arabia produces than the United States. The simplest answer to her question would be 2 million barrels more per day. But to most readers, that 2 million number is fairly meaningless. Unless they know the oil market, they have no idea whether 2 million barrels per day is a big difference or a small one.

If Saudi Arabia produced 102 million barrels of oil per day and the U.S. produced 100 million, then that 2 million-barrel difference would be rather small. Saudi Arabia would only be producing 2 percent more oil than the United States. But if 2 million were the difference between 9 million barrels in Saudi Arabia and 7 million barrels in the U.S. (which it is, approximately), then the gap would be considerably larger. It would be a 29 percent difference.

How did I arrive at 29 percent? I subtracted U.S. oil production (7 million barrels per day) from the Saudi oil production (9 million barrels per day), and then I divided that 2 million barrel-per-day difference by the U.S. figure of 7 million. The answer to the division problem is 0.29. Move the decimal two spaces to the right and, voilà, you've got a percentage: Saudi oil production is 29 percent higher than that of the U.S.

$$(9-7)/7 = 0.29$$

This same mathematical concept can be applied to population counts. Problem is, many demographers and sociologists prefer using ratios, and not percentages, when discussing gender differences in populations. U.S. colleges also use ratios to describe the gender composition of their student population. As a result, I had little choice but to also use some ratios in this book.

For me, translating a ratio into a more-than or less-than percentage is fairly intuitive, but obviously that is not true for everyone. So let's go back to 60:40, which happens to be the female-to-male sex ratio at University of North Carolina at Chapel Hill.

As I said, 60:40 means 50 percent more women than men. How did I arrive at 50 percent? One way to think of 60:40 is as a dating pool with 60 women and 40 men. In order to calculate how much bigger the female share of that dating pool is than the male one, I start by solving for the difference between 60 and 40, which is 20. To determine the percentage by which the female population exceeds the male one, I divide 20 (the difference) by 40 (the total male population). The answer is 0.50. Move the decimal two spaces to the right, and that's the percentage.

Among undergrads at UNC, there are 50 percent more women than men.

$$(60-40)/40 = 0.50$$

If you're still feeling lost, there is another way to think about ratios. 60:40 is the same as 6:4, which is the same as 3:2 (just take my word for it). If you want to visualize what 3:2 looks like, imagine you're back in college. Imagine it's late at night, and you're hanging out with friends in someone's dorm room. Imagine everyone has had a few beers, the mood is flirty, and people are thinking about pairing off.

Now imagine that there are three women and two men.

Chapter 2
How We Got to 57:43

··

Kerri Detmer* was finishing up her freshman year at Sarah Lawrence College in Bronxville, New York, when I interviewed her over coffee at Slave to the Grind, a cozy little coffee bar just off campus. A chatty 19-year-old from a small East Coast city, Detmer told me she was thriving academically at Sarah Lawrence. But socially? Not so much. Detmer knew when she applied that Sarah Lawrence's highly lopsided gender ratio might give guys the upper hand when it came to dating. "It's just as bad as I predicted," she said. "A lot of girls act like idiots around guys. I actually feel bad for the ones who didn't know what they were getting into. Some of the girls actually came here assuming Sarah Lawrence had to be fifty-fifty since it's been coed for forty years." In fact, Sarah Lawrence today is 75 percent women—which means there are three women for every one man.

Six months into her college career, Detmer had given up on finding a boyfriend on campus. Most straight men at Sarah Lawrence had no interest in a committed relationship. "Why would they?" she said. "It's like they have their own free harem. One of my friends was dumped by a guy after they'd been hooking up for less than a week. When he broke up with her, the guy actually used the word 'market'—like the 'market' for him was just too good."

The emotional toll on the women of Sarah Lawrence can range from embarrassing to traumatic. "Everyone's self-esteem takes a hit," said Detmer, who added that "the ratio" has become social shorthand among her friends—as in, "It's not your fault, it's the ratio." Her roommate suffered a minor breakdown after being rejected by a guy who had moved on to greener pastures. "She was crying hysterically and wouldn't leave his room." In an attempt to cheer the roommate up, Detmer took her to Babeland, a New York City sex shop. "I told her, 'The numbers are against us. You just need to accept that and buy a vibrator.' She got one, but it did not calm her down!" (At this point in the interview, it felt like half the coffee shop was eavesdropping.)

Of course, what is embarrassing or traumatic for Sarah Lawrence women can be the stuff of fantasy for Sarah Lawrence men (the straight ones, at least). Students there actually have an expression for guys who let their sexual good fortune go to their heads. "It's called 'Golden Cock Syndrome,'" said Jake Leventis,* a Sarah Lawrence senior whose description of campus life matched Detmer's. Leventis considered himself bisexual but added, "I mostly hook up with girls." With his rail-thin frame and unkempt beard, Leventis hardly looked like a campus Casanova. Yet it was quite clear from Leventis's explicit descriptions of social life at Sarah Lawrence that this 22-year-old was having more sex with more women than the typical college quarterback. When I asked him how many of his current female friends—just his current ones, mind you—he had had sex with, Leventis didn't bother with a mental head count. It would have taken too long. "Oh, I'd say at least twenty," Leventis answered. He did add one qualifier: "That includes a lot of threesomes and foursomes."

Leventis did not need to be told that Sarah Lawrence's over-the-top hookup culture was a by-product of there being too few men. "It's pretty clear—there isn't really a culture of monogamy or even dating here," he said. "Sometimes it feels like you can have anyone you want." From Leventis's perspective, the men at Sarah Lawrence were passive beneficiaries of the ratio rather than active exploiters. Leventis's own initiation into Sarah Lawrence's hookup culture was devoid of any sense of male entitlement, at least as he described it: "It was orientation week, and this girl came up to me, grabbed my arm, and said, 'You're going home with me tonight—got a problem with that?'"

Still, Leventis acknowledged that Sarah Lawrence women were more likely than Sarah Lawrence men to seek fidelity from their romantic partners. On account of the school's lopsided gender ratio, though, the women had little leverage. "Straight men are shared," wrote one female Sarah Lawrence blogger, "and many suffer from Golden Penis Syndrome of entitlement and manslutti-ness due to the girls they can effortlessly get on campus, some of which they wouldn't be able to get off-campus . . . [T]here are few relationships, [and] most people 'don't do labels.'"

They don't do actual dates either. "I'll go on dates sometimes—it's cute," Leventis said. "But when people talk about dating here, it's mostly just hooking up." The upshot is that Sarah Lawrence men do not have to look or act like alpha males in order to have alpha-male-like sex lives. "The hookup culture does wonders for your ego," said Leventis, "at least if you're on the right side of it."

Sarah Lawrence's gender imbalance may be extreme. Yet if you talk to women and men at some other colleges that have more women than men—and these days that's most—you will hear stories that echo those told by Detmer and Leventis. And if it has already occurred to you that the men of Sarah Lawrence sound a lot like some single, 35-year-old, college-educated men you may know in New York or Miami or even Wichita, that is no coincidence. The lopsided gender ratios on campus spilled over into the post-college dating pools years ago. Consequently, in order to understand the man deficit, you first need to go back to college.

In 1981, American colleges and universities awarded 935,140 bachelor's degrees—469,883 to men and 465,257 to women. According to the National Center for Education Statistics (NCES), that was the last time that four-year colleges in the United States graduated more men than women. Ever since, women have been leaving men in the educational dust. In 2012, women earned 1,025,729 bachelor's degrees versus just 765,317 for men (see the table on page 206). In other words, there were 34 percent more women than men who graduated from college. What's more, this gender gap is expected to grow even larger in years to come: The NCES predicted that women in the class of 2023 will outnumber men by 47 percent.

How exactly did higher education's sex ratios become so skewed? One theory is that the college man deficit is the unintended consequence of fixing an old problem in American education. Fifty years ago, there was much handwringing in the educational community about disparities that existed between girls and boys in public schools. Girls scored lower on standardized tests. Schools were setting the bar too low for female students and were doing an especially wretched job teaching them math and sciences. Discriminatory admissions policies at colleges and universities reflected a narrow-minded belief that college was often wasted on women—who supposedly went to college not to prepare for careers but to get their MRS. The college enrollment figures reflected the inequities: In 1960, men graduated from college at nearly twice the rate of women.

The passage of Title IX in 1972—banning gender discrimination at educational institutions receiving public funding—helped level the playing field. By 1982, the number of full-time, female undergraduates surpassed the number of males for the first time since World War II. But rather than plateau at 50 percent, female enrollment just kept on rising. Not only were high school girls getting better grades and improving their scores on standardized tests, but a larger share of them were applying to college in order to maximize their own future job opportunities. Whereas men with merely a high school diploma had decent opportunities to earn a middle-class wage in manufacturing or construction or the armed services, more women were seeking their entrée to the middle class by attending college.

By 1992, the female-to-male ratio among freshly minted graduates reached 54:46. At first glance, 54:46 may not sound like much of a gap, but it meant 17 percent more women than men graduating from college. When used to quantify undergraduate enrollment by sex, ratios can make gender gaps appear less significant than they actually are. To someone not well versed in mathematics or not focused on ratios' meaning, today's 65:35 female-to-male ratio at, say, Hampshire College could imply approximately one-third more women than men. In fact, 65:35 means Hampshire now has almost twice as many women as men.

By 2012, the college gender gap had doubled to 34 percent more women than men, and the gap was even wider at America's private colleges and universities. At the private institutions, women outnumbered men by nearly 50 percent—the equivalent of a 60:40 gender ratio, or three women for every two men. New York University's ratio is 61:39. Boston University's is 62:38. Tulane University in New Orleans is also 62:38. Howard University in Washington, D.C., is 69:31. Some of the most extreme college gender gaps are found at historically black institutions like Howard. Indeed, when it comes to gender gaps and their impacts, the African American community is the proverbial canary in the coal mine.

There is no question that the passage of Title IX in the U.S. helped remove barriers for female college applicants. However, the surge in female college enrollment cannot be explained primarily by Title IX, simply because the man deficit is not a uniquely American phenomenon. Women in other developed countries—Australia, Belgium, Canada, Denmark, France, Hungary, Israel, Italy, New Zealand, Spain, Sweden, the United Kingdom, etc.—also attend college in much greater numbers than men. See the table on page 207. (In England, 36 percent more women than men were accepted into four-year colleges in 2014, according to government data.) They too find themselves confronted by a post-college dating market in which men hold much of the leverage. "It's wall-to-wall arseholes out there," one 30-something Australian woman complained to a columnist for *The Sydney Morning Herald*. "I'm horrified by the number of gorgeous, independent and successful women my age who can't meet a decent man."

In hindsight, Title IX seems to have merely acceler-
ated a global trend already underway. Sixty years ago,
there was less economic incentive for high school girls to
apply to college and for women who did attend to pursue
career-oriented degrees. A key driver of gains in female
college enrollment, according to Harvard University
economist Claudia Goldin, is the expectation of future
labor force participation. Interestingly, the college wage
premium—the excess wages one earns thanks to a college diploma—has always been higher for women than
for men. But back in the 1950s, when women were typically getting married by age 21 or 22 and having children
soon thereafter, the college wage premium was basically
irrelevant to most women since they did not anticipate
long stays in the workforce. High school girls were less
inclined to take college-track courses in math and sciences (and hence scored lower on standardized tests), and
women who did go to college sometimes gave short shrift
to their studies. "Because the age at first marriage was so
low," Goldin and coauthors Lawrence Katz and Ilyana
Kuziemko wrote in a 2006 paper, "a young woman who
had not secured a husband while she was in college would
have been rather tense, possibly panicky, at graduation. In
consequence, college was often taken less seriously."

So what changed in the 1960s and 1970s? The usual
suspects are feminism and the passage of federal anti-
discrimination laws like Title IX and the Equal Pay Act
of 1963. But as I said, women began attending college
in greater numbers not just in the U.S. but all across the

developed world—even in countries where women's push for equal rights evolved more slowly. Goldin offered a much different explanation, one driven by a much different kind of catalyst. She credited the pill.

The contraceptive pill was first introduced in 1960, and by the end of the decade it had morphed into a pharmaceutical and social phenomenon—landing on the cover of *Time* magazine in 1967. Oral contraceptives gave women control over family planning and allowed them to delay marriage and spend more time in the workforce. "The widespread legality and acceptance of the 'pill' as a birth control device," Goldin and her coauthors wrote, "allowed young women to plan their futures more accurately and also helped facilitate a large increase in the age at first marriage." Delayed marriage and childbearing allowed greater investment in careers and thus in higher education as well. In economic terms, the pill lowered the true cost of attending college by increasing the likelihood that a college degree would pay financial dividends in the future.

The widespread popularity of the pill helps explain why women caught up to men in college enrollment. Yet it cannot explain why women blew right by men over the ensuing thirty years, with women now graduating from college in 34 percent greater numbers. From today's vantage point, it appears that the old disincentives and discrimination confronting high school girls obscured a fundamental biological truth: Girls have a developmental advantage when it comes to college preparation. Girls mature earlier—behaviorally and intellectually—and thus get better grades in school, spend more time on homework, have fewer disciplinary problems, are less prone to criminality, and are two to three times less likely to be diagnosed with attention deficit hyperactivity disorder (ADHD). Girls and boys may score comparably on intelligence tests, but because of maturity differences, girls fare better when it comes to actual schoolwork.

A 2000 study led by Washington University neuroscientist Andrey Anokhin found that girls' brains were more mature than boys' brains from age 7 to 17 and that the differential widened into the teen years. University of Michigan education professor Brian Jacob found in 2002 that girls' more advanced social skills—specifically, their superior ability to pay attention in class, to work with others, and to organize and keep track of homework—contributed heavily to the gender gap in college enrollment. In 2012, 70 percent of U.S. high school valedictorians were girls, according to news reports. A 2004 government survey out of the U.K. found that 78 percent of girls age 11 to 16 completed all their homework regularly, versus only 61 percent of boys. A 2013 study by the U.S. Centers for Disease Control found that 15 percent of school-age boys had received an ADHD diagnosis (versus just 7 percent for girls), a diagnosis rate so over the top that some researchers believe simple immaturity is now being misdiagnosed as ADHD. "There's a tremendous push where if the kid's behavior is thought to be quote-unquote abnormal—if they're not sitting quietly at their desk—that's pathological, instead of just childhood," Jerome

Groopman, a professor at Harvard Medical School, told *The New York Times*.

For Goldin and her coauthors, the bottom line was clear: "Because gender differences in development and behavior are not unique to any particular country, they explain why the reversal of the gender gap in college has occurred throughout much of the developed world once female access to college and to labor market opportunities were improved." (Boys' slower development relative to girls hints at one way to reduce the man deficit. More on that in the final chapter.)

Along with the developmental issues holding some boys back from college, there are economic forces at play too. For example, according to the U.S. Bureau of Labor Statistics, the fastest-growing profession in the country is nursing. Nursing happens to be a profession dominated by women, and because nursing generally requires a college degree, high demand for nurses translates to more women attending college. (College nursing programs are generally more than 80 percent women.)

There are also greater opportunities for men than for women to earn a decent wage right out of high school, which is why the college wage premium for women is significantly higher. In the booming oil fields of North Dakota and Texas, for example, it is not uncommon for 19-year-old roughnecks—almost all of them men—to pull in upward of $60,000 a year. Nationally, the average pay for high school–educated men is $31,730 a year versus only $21,682 for high school–educated women, according to Census Bureau data. And according to a different set of data from NCES, 28 percent of men with only a high school diploma earn more than $50,000 a year, versus just 9 percent of such women. Over the long haul, men would still be better off going to college—61 percent of college-educated men earn $50,000 a year or more. But in the short term, better job opportunities do seem to draw more men into the blue-collar workforce straight out of high school.

Of course, if economics and biology are behind the college gender gap—and not some type of reverse discrimination against men—it begs the question of whether the college gender gap is actually a problem in need of a solution. In other words, should we even care that fewer men than women attend college? When I posed this question to Goldin, her answer was an emphatic no. "I don't see any obvious reason to worry about it," Goldin said. "There aren't any impediments or hurdles or barriers or prejudices or discriminatory factors or regulations standing in the way [of men going to college]."

Bernice Sandler, the celebrated women's rights advocate who was the driving force behind the passage of Title IX, gave me much the same answer. "No, the idea of a college is to educate people," Sandler told me. "When you choose between people to come to the college, you choose the people who are most likely to benefit from it." Sandler went so far as to cast doubt on the notion that female-heavy gender ratios have any negative impact on college life. "Students don't notice the difference," Sandler said. "In a large college, you're never going to know [that there are more women than men]."

It is hard to argue with Sandler's logic about college existing primarily for education, not for finding a girlfriend or boyfriend or spouse. But her suggestion that college students "don't notice" the gender gap is, to be frank, ridiculous. Not only are students keenly aware of the gender gap, but it is also a source of distress for women who are ostensibly benefiting from attending college in greater numbers than men. Consider this excerpt from the aforementioned 2010 *New York Times* article on the social impact that 60:40 gender ratios are having at large public universities such as University of North Carolina at Chapel Hill:

> *Jayne Dallas, a senior studying advertising [at UNC], grumbled that the population of male undergraduates was even smaller when you looked at it as a dating pool. "Out of that 40 percent, there are maybe 20 percent that we would consider, and out of those 20, 10 have girlfriends, so all the girls are fighting over that other 10 percent," she said.*
>
> *Needless to say, this puts guys in a position to play the field, and tends to mean that even the ones willing to make a commitment come with storied romantic histories. Rachel Sasser, a senior history major at the table, said that before she and her boyfriend started dating, he had "hooked up with at least five of my friends in my sorority—that I know of . . ."*

Thanks to simple laws of supply and demand, it is often the women who must assert themselves romantically or be left alone on Valentine's Day, staring down a George Clooney movie over a half-empty pizza box.

"I was talking to a friend at a bar, and this girl just came up out of nowhere, grabbed him by the wrist, spun him around, and took him out to the dance floor and started grinding," said Kelly Lynch, a junior at North Carolina, recalling a recent experience . . .

"A lot of my friends will meet someone and go home for the night and just hope for the best the next morning," Ms. Lynch said. "They'll text them and say: 'I had a great time. Want to hang out next week?' And they don't respond."

Even worse, "Girls feel pressured to do more than they're comfortable with, to lock it down," Ms. Lynch said.

Mental health professionals who provide counseling and psychological services at colleges have noticed too. Brunhild Kring, associate director of counseling and wellness services at New York University, has raised red flags about the no-strings-attached sexual culture taking root at NYU and other colleges with 60:40 gender ratios. "In the last two decades the gender ratio among college students has dramatically shifted," Kring wrote in a 2012 article published in the *Journal of the Eastern Group*

Psychotherapy Society. "Women outnumber men by a ratio of 60:40, and a new sexual paradigm has emerged . . . '[D]ating' in the traditional sense of the word had been replaced by 'hooking up' as the predominant premarital sexual interaction on college campus." This, Kring concluded, can contribute to emotional "confusion" and "a loss of direction" among students.

To illustrate her point, Kring recounted the story of a 20-year-old woman who came to her for counseling following a night of drinking and unprotected sex. According to Kring, the young woman reported that she had "lost her virginity in a threesome by hooking up in an alcohol-fueled night of partying with a gay and a straight male student." The young woman was too intoxicated at the time of the encounter to remember exactly what had happened—other than the fact that she woke up next to another woman, who had also passed out. Eventually, one of the men with whom the woman had had sex returned to the apartment and filled her in on precisely what had occurred: "The student believes that she had vaginal and anal intercourse, but that 'no one had come,'" Kring wrote.

"I listened to her story with trepidation," Kring continued, "concerned that this experience would turn out to be upsetting and traumatic to her. But after she had gone over the sexual interchanges with her gay friend, she felt proud of herself. Tall for a woman, she had thought of herself as unattractive and had given up hope of finding a romantic partner. Now she had gloriously lost her virginity in a threesome. Immediately, she got onto Skype to confide in her two closest girlfriends back home. They were impressed that this hoped-for rite of passage had finally taken place in such cinematic circumstances."

The young woman's initial excitement proved short-lived. Indeed, a study published by five Loyola Marymount University psychologists found that college women were twice as likely as college men to experience psychological distress after hookups. "Critical judgment had set in and the student decided to come to the Health Center," Kring wrote. "She felt awkward and wanted help in keeping her sexual encounter private from other students. I also referred her for an immediate sexual health and contraceptive visit with the Women's Center."

This is not to say that all college women are pressured into the hookup culture or that college women would never choose to have casual sex if their odds of finding a boyfriend were better. A much talked about *New York Times* article from 2013 told the hookup-culture story from the perspective of University of Pennsylvania women who said they were putting their energies into academics, internships, and preparing for careers—and not relationships. For the UPenn women, choosing hookups over boyfriends boiled down to a time-management strategy.

Hailee Katz, the sexually adventurous young college grad quoted earlier, expressed similar sentiments. In the wake of back-to-back relationships, Katz told me she had decided to take a breather from boyfriends. "To be honest, I hated it," Katz said of being in a relationship. "It was exhausting. Every other night I was out with these guys. I had less time for work. I never made it to yoga. I never saw my friends. I never cleaned my apartment. I never got anything done."

It's progress that millennial women can now enjoy the occasional (or more-than-occasional) one-night stand with minimal social stigma. It's a good thing that they now can decide for themselves how they want to prioritize sex versus romance—a luxury their own mothers may not have had. In *The End of Men*, Rosin goes so far as to celebrate the benefits to women of the hookup culture, comparing it to "an island" young women visit when they're young and experimenting and adventuresome, one that doesn't distract from "more important things" such as grades and career.

Young people should just be aware, though, that lopsided gender ratios make Hookup Island a different place for men than for women—and not just because men lack biological clocks. Katz's notion that hooking up is fun when you're young but sad when you're old assumes that she'll be able to transition seamlessly from casual sex to serious relationships. Thing is, the longer men stay on Hookup Island, the better it becomes for them. For women not interested in marriage, this mating math probably doesn't matter, but it could matter to women who aim to get married and start a family eventually. Just imagine Hookup Island starts out with a pool of 14 women and 10 men. Once 6 of the men and 6 of the women settle down together and opt to return to the Monogamy Mainland, the remaining dating pool on Hookup Island becomes 8 women and 4 men—a true male paradise.

There's also a chicken-or-the-egg element to deciphering the origins of the relaxed attitudes toward sex exhibited by young women like Katz and by the UPenn students interviewed by the *Times*. Are these women putting dating and marriage on the back burner simply because they enjoy casual sex and because they feel less burdened by sexual stigma than previous generations of women? Or, alternatively, has the man deficit discouraged college-educated women from putting too high a priority on love and romance because love and romance are now harder to come by?

Even if colleges and universities wanted to balance their gender gaps, there are no simple ways for administrators to accomplish this. Public colleges and universities cannot lower admissions standards for men without violating Title IX. Private colleges do have a Title IX exemption for admissions, but given campus politics—not to mention the likelihood that increasing male enrollment might require cuts to women's athletics—it is hard to imagine many college presidents publicly embracing the idea of affirmative action for men. (Under Title IX, sports participation is supposed to mirror campus gender ratios.) Fully aware of this, I still wanted to ask NYU president John Sexton if he had any *in loco parentis*-type concerns about the connection between his school's 61:39 gender ratio and the hookup culture among undergrads that so concerned Kring. Sexton declined my interview request through a spokesman.

Sexton is a law professor by training, so it is possible he is unaware of the social science linking gender ratios to sexual behavior. One college president whom I knew was well acquainted with gender-ratio research is Teresa Sullivan, president of 56 percent female University of Virginia. Sullivan is a former sociology professor who used to teach *Too Many Women?: The Sex Ratio Question*—the pioneering book on the perverse effects of lopsided gender ratios—in her own class. Sullivan even reviewed *Too Many Women?* for an academic journal ("interesting and provocative" was her assessment), so I knew that Sullivan understood the connection between the 27 percent oversupply of women at UVA and the school's well-publicized hookup culture (a culture thrust into the spotlight in the wake of *Rolling Stone*'s since-discredited UVA rape story from 2014).

Some of Sullivan's students and faculty had made this connection on their own. "Because there are so many females, the men get to set the norms," said UVA senior Elliot Johnson in a 2013 story in *The Cavalier Daily* about the campus hookup culture. UVA politics professor Steven Rhoads was even more explicit in an article—titled "Hookup Culture: The High Costs of a Low 'Price' for Sex"—that he penned in 2012 for the scholarly journal *Society*. Rhoads's paper included this quote from a female undergrad: "I hate this feeling—the pressure to sell my body to men, to dress scandalously just to get their attention, just to get them to notice me. Then all they want is a one-night stand; they will use me for sex and don't give a shit about me as a person."

I had hoped that Sullivan, a sociologist who understands the impact of skewed gender ratios, would want to speak out on this issue. But just like Sexton, Sullivan declined to talk with me.

College presidents' reluctance to discuss the gender gap came as no surprise to Bruce Poch, former dean of admissions at Pomona College in Claremont, California. "This issue is sufficiently explosive that most college presidents would rather run and hide than address it," explained Poch, now the dean of admissions and executive director of college counseling at Chadwick, a Los Angeles prep school. Wary of reputational damage, colleges don't want to acknowledge the role they've inadvertently played in fostering the hookup culture on their campuses, Poch said. Perhaps more to the point: "They certainly don't want to get into a Title IX fight over admitting more boys."

For colleges and universities, acknowledging the connection between gender ratios and the hookup culture could prove embarrassing. Nevertheless, transparency is the first step toward addressing the problem. Men and women will adjust to imbalances in the dating market if those imbalances are visible and understood. If college-bound boys and girls were told that the hookup culture is more extreme at a 60:40 school like NYU with three women for every two men, perhaps more boys would apply there and perhaps more girls would opt for other selective colleges that offer greater gender balance—such as Johns Hopkins, Tufts, or Georgia Tech.

(Colleges and universities with larger math and sciences departments generally attract more men.)

Similarly, if 15-year-old boys who are borderline candidates for even attending college were presented with better information about the two life paths before them—a working-class dating pool with too many men versus a college-educated one with too many women—perhaps more of those boys would study harder in high school. "Absolutely, I could see that," said a guidance counselor at a midsize public high school in North Carolina. "Social factors are huge. For some boys, it's a motivating factor for why they even come to school." The problem—and the reason this guidance counselor wanted to remain anonymous—is that no high school guidance counselor who wanted to keep her job would ever dream of telling a teenage boy that he should improve his grades so he can go to a school like UNC Chapel Hill and hook up with a new girl every week.

"We just show them the numbers," the guidance counselor said. "The rest they have to figure out for themselves."

Chapter 3
Sex Ratios 101

···

Joshua Ackerman is a psychologist who teaches at the Massachusetts Institute of Technology's Sloan School of Management. What is a shrink doing at an elite business school, one best known for developing complex financial formulas such as the Black-Scholes model for pricing options? While Ackerman's training may be in psychology, rest assured that the professor's interests are thoroughly capitalistic.

Soft-spoken and bearing a slight resemblance to actor Noah Wyle (albeit with many flecks more gray hair), Ackerman teaches marketing at Sloan. He uses the tools of social psychology to analyze consumer behavior. Ackerman's research sometimes converges on the interplay between gender, romance, and child rearing on one behavioral axis and spending, saving, and responsiveness to marketing on the other. Consequently, Ackerman is *extremely* interested in the role that gender ratios play in shaping consumer choices.

I will return a little later to Ackerman's specific findings, but what struck me most when I spoke with him at his MIT office was the way Ackerman described the intellectual foundation of his research. Ackerman's starting point was not economics or management theory or any other traditional business-school discipline. It was evolutionary biology. "You can get a lot of ideas on how people make decisions by looking at the literature on animal behavior," Ackerman explained. "Many of the ways we as humans think about things are very, very similar to what animals do. And one of those ideas where there's been a lot of work done in the animal literature involves the concept of sex ratios."

Turns out, many of the dating customs observed in the coffee shops of Sunnyvale, California, the honky tonks of Dallas, and the wine bars of Manhattan's Upper East Side have their roots in nature. Consider the behavior of pond cichlids, a species of fish that is typically monogamous during mating season. When zoologists experimented with altering sex ratios in a controlled population of cichlids, even small manipulations had profound impacts on the male cichlids' likelihood of staying committed to their female mates.

Increasing the ratio of male cichlids to females

from 6:6 to 7:5 cut the male desertion rate in half—from 22 percent to 11 percent. It also rendered females choosier about males and made the successful male suitors more protective of their females. The end result was a kind of underwater patriarchy—one in which male cichlids fought each other for access to mates, jealously guarded their females after mating, and then, after the fry were born, made greater investments in parenting (be it through direct parenting effort or via the providing of resources such as food or protection).

Some of these behavioral patterns are surely quite familiar to anyone who has spent time in nightclubs, dive bars, or other spots where single men and women routinely socialize. Like the male cichlids, men get reflexively more protective of "their" women when more men enter the physical space.

A more surprising finding from the animal studies involved what happened when sex ratios were manipulated to make the females more plentiful. For the cichlids, a decrease in male-to-female sex ratios from 6:6 to 5:7 yielded a hugely disproportionate behavioral response. Male desertion rates more than doubled—from 22 percent to 51 percent. In other words, a seemingly small shift in the female share of the cichlid population transformed the prevailing mating culture from one of monogamy to one of polygyny, which is males mating with multiple females but females mating with only one male. "Males increasingly deserted their mates and the young in their care as the opportunity to re-mate increased in their environment," wrote Mart Gross, a University of Toronto zoology professor, in an article published in 2005.

Presumably male cichlids do not act this way out of piscine malice or misogyny. They do it because it is biologically rational. A goal for males of all species is to pass along their genes to the next generation. When sex ratios are balanced or are lopsided in favor of more males, males have a strong genetic incentive to stick with their original mates and to actively participate in the care and protection of young. When females are more abundant, however, the mating game shifts in favor of the male having multiple broods. Even if one or more broods are abandoned by the male and left vulnerable to predators, the male cichlid is still likely to produce more offspring overall. In such an environment, male reproductive strategies tend to emphasize mating effort at the expense of parenting effort, simply because the value of monogamy declines as the ratio of males to females declines. In nature, when females are plentiful, natural selection favors those males that mate with more than one female.

The consensus among animal scientists is that male behavior is more influenced by changes in sex ratios than female behavior is. Yet females are not impervious to mating-market supply and demand. When males are widely available, females are more likely to seek out the largest, strongest potential mates. "In resource-based mating systems, it has been relatively straightforward to show that females prefer males that provide the most resources such as food, shelter, parental care, and protection from predators," according to biologists Bryan Neff of the University of Western Ontario and Trevor Pitcher of the University of Windsor. On the other hand, when males are the scarcer sex, females not only become less choosy about males but are also forced to compete with each other for access to them.

Consider a species of seabird known as the red phalarope. Red phalaropes are unusual in the avian world, as it is males, not females, that bear responsibility for incubating eggs and rearing hatchlings. On account of their parental responsibilities, a significant percentage of male red phalaropes are usually sexually unavailable to the females—creating what scientists describe as a "low operational sex ratio." There may be just as many male red phalaropes as females in the overall population, but the net effect of the sex-role reversal is a functional shortage of males. As a result, the seabirds' courtship patterns become role-reversed too.

Female red phalaropes fight among themselves for mates. And in one study of the birds' mating behavior conducted by John Reynolds and Fred Cooke of Queens University in Ontario, and Mark Colwell of the University of North Dakota, females that had yet to secure a mate routinely "harassed" newly bonded mating pairs, presumably in an attempt to break up the pairs and steal a mate. The key takeaway from such studies is clear: "Across a huge variety of species, the sex ratio in a breeding population is the most important environmental factor affecting mating patterns in nominally monogamous species," according to Boise State University sociologist Anthony Walsh.

Acknowledging this evolutionary reality does not mean excusing the behavior of humans who engage in philandering, two-timing, gold-digging, or home-wrecking. People, unlike animals, have a moral compass—an ability to rise above our baser instincts. There's also great value in coming to grips with the fact that some of our behavior is instinctive rather than learned. As a financial writer, I know just how empowering such knowledge can be. My friend Jason Zweig, a former *Money* magazine colleague who now writes for *The Wall Street Journal*, reminds his readers all the time that they must resist natural inclinations in order to become smarter investors. An expert in behavioral finance, Zweig points out that humans have an all-too-powerful panic reflex, one that evolved at a time when escaping bad weather and avoiding predators were foremost concerns for prehistoric man. "[T]he amygdala—the part of your brain that initiates feelings of fear—is an almost irresistible force," Zweig wrote in *Money* in 2002. Our brains are hardwired to overreact, which is why Zweig cautions investors against bailing on promising stocks after one poor quarter or one scary headline.

Once investors are made aware of irrational or inefficient behavior, they are more likely to change their ways. Consider the saga of the January Effect. Back in the 1940s, academics and money managers began to observe an annual trading pattern in which stocks sold off in late

December only to rebound in early January. The reason? Investors were selling their money-losing stocks at the end of the year in order to create accounting losses that could then be used to reduce income taxes. After January 1—once the tax losses were locked in—they bought the stocks back.

For a while, the January Effect was a boon to stock market insiders who understood what was going on and thus were able to pick up stocks on the cheap in December and then flip them for quick profits come January. There was just one problem. Those making money off the January Effect did not keep their secret to themselves. They gave interviews. They wrote journal articles. And it was publicity that ultimately killed the January Effect. As more and more investors bought stocks in December, they bid up the prices of shares that otherwise would have been depressed by tax-related selling. "Indeed, the January Effect became undependable after it received considerable publicity," Princeton University economist Burton Malkiel wrote in *A Random Walk Down Wall Street*. "[A]ny truly repetitive and exploitable pattern that can be discovered in the stock market and can be arbitraged away will self-destruct."

Baseball fans who read Michael Lewis's *Moneyball* are well acquainted with the concept of publicity destroying exploitable patterns. It was not long after Lewis popularized the fact that hitters with high on-base percentages were undervalued that the cost of acquiring such hitters via the free agent market soared.

I believe a similar fate awaits the college gender gap and the man deficit in the post-college dating market. Man deficits will shrink and eventually vanish as gender ratios and their effects become exposed and publicized, and as men and women adapt to new information.

Although biologists and zoologists have been studying animal sex ratios since the days of Charles Darwin, the pioneering scholarly work on *human* gender ratios was not published until 1983. *Too Many Women?: The Sex Ratio Question*—the book that UVA president Teresa Sullivan used to assign to her sociology class—was the brainchild of psychologist Marcia Guttentag, a professor at Harvard University. The book was completed and coauthored by Paul Secord, Guttentag's second husband and a professor at the University of Houston, following Guttentag's sudden death in 1977 at the age of 44.

Too Many Women's big idea was an audacious one— "that the number of opposite-sex partners potentially available to men or women has profound effects on sexual behaviors and sexual mores, on patterns of marriage and divorce, childrearing conditions and practices, family stability, and certain structural aspects of society itself." A psychologist and academic on the front lines of the feminist movement, Guttentag found herself struggling to understand a sudden rise in suicide and depression among young women in the 1960s and 1970s. Her epiphany came, oddly enough, after a night at the opera.

In the preface of *Too Many Women*, Guttentag recalls taking her teenage daughter, Lisa, to see Mozart's *The Magic Flute* performed in English and then being thunderstruck by the lyrics. Guttentag notes how each of the male protagonists "sings of his determination to find a wife and of his longing to make a commitment to a woman for life . . . The intensity of their desire is demonstrated by their willingness to undergo severe trials in order to enter Sarastro's brotherhood and claim their respective loves." Curious, Guttentag asked her daughter if she noticed anything odd about the lyrics. Her daughter's response: The lyrics were "strange" because the men sang "about wanting to make a lifelong commitment to one woman—a wife."

Both mother and daughter observed similarities between *The Magic Flute* and the idealized depiction of women in popular American songs of the 1930s, '40s, and '50s—before America's gender ratio swung from more men than women to more women than men. (Prior to World War II, immigrants to the U.S. were disproportionately male.) Guttentag grew up in the 1930s and '40s, and the pop lyrics of Guttentag's youth had always emphasized "romantic love, exclusive commitment for life, marriage, and monogamy." By the 1960s and '70s, however, music's romantic themes had given way to a more sexualized "'love 'em and leave 'em' ethos." In contemporary lyrics, she observed, "there was no sign of a male's intention to make a long-term sexual commitment, and marriage was never mentioned."

Why? Guttentag wondered. "Why the difference between Mozart's lyrics two centuries ago and our lyrics today?" One striking possibility came to mind: "Are there too many unattached women? Is there actually a shortage of men? If there is, could this possibly explain *all* of these changes?"

Guttentag was onto something. As she and Secord would show, the national sex ratio for marriage-age Americans swung from more men to more women during the decade intervening the 1960 and 1970 censuses. Back then, women typically married men three or four years their senior, and the post–World War II Baby Boom meant there were many more women born in 1946, 1947, and 1948 than there were men born in 1943, 1944, and 1945. On account of this—and on account of the generally rising number of births from 1945 through 1957—American women born in this era got caught in what would later be known as "the marriage squeeze." A dating market that had been 111 marriage-age men for every 100 marriage-age women in 1960 evolved into one with 84 men for every 100 women in 1970, according to Guttentag and Secord.

In order to understand the implications of this demographic shift, Guttentag spent years poring through Census numbers, sex-ratio data, and other historical materials dating all the way back to ancient Greece and medieval Europe. Her and Secord's conclusions? In societies in which men outnumbered women, the prevailing culture was more likely to emphasize romance and courtship. Men must compete for a wife and thus they were more willing to make and to keep a commitment to remain with her. And while women in such societies did tend to play rather stereotypical roles of "homemaker and mother," the high ratios of men to women gave women the power to "choose among men for a marriage partner." This, Guttentag and Secord concluded, "gives women a subjective sense of power and control" since they are highly valued by men as "romantic love objects."

The story changed, though, when the women outnumbered the men—just as it did in the animal kingdom. When men were the ones in undersupply, women were "more likely to be valued as mere sex objects," according to Guttentag and Secord. One upside for everyone was that the quality and variety of sex seemed to improve. Clinical sex studies observed "a real increase in and diversification of erotic activity" as twentieth-century gender ratios began to skew female, they wrote. "Coital frequency and length of intercourse have both increased substantially, as has length of foreplay."

A second upside: Historically, when men were scarce, women were more likely to attain political rights and economic parity. For example, in ancient Sparta, where the ratio of men to women was low, women were highly educated and controlled two-fifths of land and property.

For women, however, the advantages associated with too few men did not erase the problem of diminished marriage prospects. In the too-many-women societies, the culture did not emphasize love and commitment, Guttentag and Secord concluded. Sex outside of marriage became the norm and out-of-wedlock births commonplace. "The outstanding characteristic of times when women were in oversupply would be that men would *not* remain committed to the same woman throughout her childbearing years." More men and women remained single because men had less incentive to settle down. And when couples did marry, they were more likely to get divorced.

For men and women alike, "sexual libertarianism" became "the prevailing ethos" of the day. "Brief liaisons would be usual, as men would have opportunities to move successively from woman to woman or to maintain multiple relationships with different women."

Sound familiar?

For Guttentag, the implications of shifting sex ratios were both historical—she believed the sexual revolution and the feminist movement were fueled by lopsided gender ratios—and personal too. Divorced in her twenties, Guttentag spent much of her adult life as a single mother balancing kids and career. "Her first husband walked out on her," said Susan Salasin, one of Guttentag's closest friends.

In theory, Guttentag should not have had much trouble remarrying. According to Salasin and others, Guttentag was attractive, kind, charismatic, and brilliant. One of her former research assistants at Harvard, Kit Wheatley, said Guttentag was extremely popular with students. Yet dating proved to be a major struggle for Guttentag—more so, it seemed, than for divorcées of her mother's generation. "She had trouble finding another man," said her son Michael Guttentag, now a law professor. "I think she was really struck by how poorly the men treated women back then. There seemed to be a lack of chivalry."

In this context, Guttentag's gender-ratio-driven theory explaining the rise of feminism in the 1960s and 1970s has an almost autobiographical tinge. "Why," she and Secord wrote, "should women in these contemporary times be fighting so hard for power, independence, and equality? Why should they feel that they have been used, manipulated, exploited, and cast aside? Although they are far from having status and power equal to that of men, women have been vastly more oppressed in other times and places than they are in America today. Is it only that they are more aware of the inequalities, and in a better position to fight for more equal standing? Or is there something more that contributes to the surge of feminism in these contemporary times?"

According to Guttentag and Secord, the sexual revolution, the increased depression rates among young women, and the women's movement itself were all by-products of lopsided gender ratios: "What we are suggesting in answer to the sex ratio question is that, given the abundance of unattached women, men will shape to their advantage the form that relationships between men and women take. With a surplus of women, sexual freedoms are more advantageous to men than to women. Decreased willingness to commit oneself to an exclusive relationship with one woman is consistent with that fact . . . It follows further that the persistence of such circumstances would leave many women hurt and angry. Other women, not themselves without a man, would nevertheless often be aware of the unfortunate experiences of their women friends in relations with men. These circumstances should impel women to seek more power and, incidentally, turn them toward meeting their own needs. Most forms of feminism are directed to just such ends."

To be sure, the conditions observed 40 years ago by Guttentag are materially different from those that exist today. Back then, the gender-ratio imbalance was caused by the combined effects of the Baby Boom and the traditional age gap at marriage; the resulting "marriage squeeze" transcended social class. Today's man deficit is a by-product of the widening gender gap in college enrollment, which means it affects white-collar populations differently than blue-collar ones. Nevertheless, the cultural impact of too many women remains the same. The sexual revolution that so interested Guttentag and the hookup culture now running rampant in college and post-college dating markets are both rooted in a statistical oversupply of women.

Marcia Guttentag deserved far more recognition than she ever received for explaining phenomena that caused others to throw up their hands in kids-these-days type frustration. Secord wrote that *Too Many Women?* was supposed to be Guttentag's "letter to the world." Salasin told me Guttentag was convinced *Too*

Many Women? would be a blockbuster. "She definitely thought the book would be a big deal," added Michael Guttentag. Unfortunately, *Too Many Women?* never became the cultural touchstone Guttentag hoped for, probably because she was not alive to promote the book or to continue her sex-ratio research.

Nevertheless, *Too Many Women?* did leave its mark in scholarly circles. Famed political scientist James Q. Wilson used it to help explain the decline of marriage in the inner city. Katherine Trent and Scott South, sociology professors at University of Albany-SUNY, found that marriage rates are higher and divorce rates lower in countries where men outnumber women. (Trent and South's thesis seemingly applies to U.S. states too. Hawaii, for instance, has 17 percent more men than women age 20 to 34, thanks to its eleven U.S. military bases. Not coincidentally, Hawaii boasts a marriage rate for women that is 5 percentage points higher than the national average.)

Evolutionary psychologist Nigel Barber discovered that countries with high ratios of men to women have lower teen pregnancy rates. In another study, Barber analyzed crime data from Interpol and found a correlation between low numbers of men and high rates of sexual assault. Elevated rape rates were "a predictable feature of countries with a relative scarcity of men," according to Barber. Robert O'Brien, a sociology professor at University of Oregon, studied U.S. crime data and reached the same conclusion. Drawing on Guttentag and Secord, O'Brien theorized that men are more likely to "protect their women" when women are in short supply. (Guttentag and Secord had noted that the punishment for rape in ancient Greece was far harsher in city-states with oversupplies of men versus those with oversupplies of women—death in Athens compared to a monetary fine in Sparta.) Given the recent spate of high-profile campus rape cases, Barber's and O'Brien's research begs the question of whether colleges' lopsided sex ratios may be indirectly contributing to a rise in campus sexual assaults. It's a question that universities with big gender imbalances should surely be investigating.

More recently, younger academics have built upon Guttentag's research to explain social and economic changes now impacting marriage-age men and women here in the U.S. and all across the globe. Writing in *Sociological Quarterly* in 2010, sociology professors Jeremy Uecker of Baylor University and Mark Regnerus of University of Texas at Austin showed that women attending colleges with 60:40 ratios of women to men were significantly more likely to be sexually active and significantly less likely to have gone out on more than six traditional dates during their college careers (versus merely "hooking up"), as compared to women attending schools that were only 47 percent women. On the 40 percent–female campuses, women with boyfriends were also substantially more likely to remain virgins.

"Women who attend college on campuses where they are more numerous tend to view men as less interested in commitment and less trustworthy," Uecker and Regnerus wrote in a paper that they eventually turned into a book (one popular with some conservatives, thanks to the book's anti–casual sex tilt and also to Regnerus's opposition to same-sex marriage). "They are less likely to expect much from men, find it more difficult to locate the right kind of men, and are more likely to report that their relationships don't work out and that a woman can't have a boyfriend if she won't have sex . . . It appears men behave differently in different relationship markets."

In order to test the idea that men and women behave differently in different relationship markets, I paid a visit to the California Institute of Technology in Pasadena, California, and conducted a focus group with a dozen CalTech undergrads, a few of whom I had already interviewed by phone. CalTech intrigued me because it is one of only a handful of major non-religious universities in the U.S. where men comprise a significant majority. CalTech's gender ratio among undergrads is 59:41 *men* to *women*.

One of the things I learned was that at CalTech, "hookups" are not even part of the vernacular. "The guys are never going to get a situation where they're hooking up every night, because the girls just won't go for that," said Kathy Li.* CalTech students go out on real dates and have actual boyfriends and girlfriends. "If people do get involved, it's always in a relationship," said Graham Simmons.* "The couples tend to be connected at the hip."

The CalTech dating culture may sound like a throwback, but it is a perfect example of how dating behavior varies depending upon market conditions. Just as

Guttentag and Secord theorized, the oversupply of men at CalTech does indeed lead to greater emphasis on courtship and romance. Simmons mentioned an annual Valentine's Day tradition at Lloyd House, his CalTech residence, that was equal parts adorable and flabbergasting. He said the Lloyd men prepare for Valentine's Day by making hand-crafted Valentines for all the Lloyd women, and then they wake up at the crack of dawn on Valentine's Day morning to cook the women pancakes.

Male and female CalTech students alike told me it is not uncommon for couples that begin dating freshman year to stay together through all four years of college. One woman said that at the start of her freshman year, a resident advisor in her dorm actually counseled her not to rush into her first college relationship: "She told me, 'You'll probably end up marrying the guy.'" CalTech does not keep statistics on how many alums are married to each other, but alumni relations director Alexx Tobeck did tell me she knows there are "a lot."

For the record, the reason the dating culture at CalTech sounds old-fashioned is not because the students there are all geeks. The hookup culture is alive and well at equally brainy Massachusetts Institute of Technology, according to Christine Yu, a 2012 grad and former sex columnist for the MIT student newspaper. Much like CalTech, MIT has more men then women (though at 55:45 men to women, MIT's gender ratio is less lopsided). However, MIT's dating scene plays differently, Yu told me, due to the large number of Wellesley College women who take classes at MIT and who attend MIT parties, and also due to MIT's physical proximity to Boston University, which is 62 percent female.

Statistics culled from the online dating site OkCupid provided further evidence that gender ratios shape college social life. Analyzing colleges by the sexual appetites of their students, OkCupid's OkTrends data blog identified the horniest colleges in America as Sarah Lawrence (no surprise there) and University of Vermont. The rankings were based on how many times a week students stated in their dating profiles that they wanted to have sex. At both Sarah Lawrence and UVM, the average response was six. While OkTrends did not link these findings to gender ratios—the blog was trying to connect sexual behavior to tuition rates—it is hard to overlook gender ratios as a contributing factor. UVM, with a 59:41 ratio, has approximately three women for every two men (students at the Burlington campus refer to it as Girlington), while Sarah Lawrence has three women for every one man, according to U.S. Department of Education data compiled by StudentAdvisor.com.

What about the schools at the bottom of the OkCupid's preferred-amount-of-intercourse-per-week rankings? Well, among colleges included in the OkCupid survey (CalTech was not included), the two least horny schools were both majority male—Iowa State (54 percent male) and Texas A&M (51 percent male).

Research also suggests that Sarah Lawrence and University of Vermont women who do land boyfriends may have had to lower their standards. A 2011 study in the academic journal *Animal Behaviour* found that women's preference for male facial symmetry—a key determinant of attractiveness—varies depending upon women's perception of prevailing gender ratios. Christopher Watkins, a lecturer at Abertay University in the U.K., and four other researchers from the U.K. and Canada, conducted a three-stage experiment in which 100 women with a median age of 23 were shown head shots of 10 young men and 10 young women. For each of the head shots, there were two side-by-side, identical-looking versions of the same photo—the original, and another in which the image had been photoshopped to create facial symmetry. Not told that one of the seemingly identical photos had been photoshopped, the women in the study were asked to express a preference for either the original or the symmetrical version.

In the second stage of the experiment, participants were shown a slide show of 30 new faces. Half the participants were shown a slide show in which 25 out of the 30 new images were male faces, while the other half were shown one in which 25 out of 30 were female faces. In the third stage of the experiment, the participants were asked to repeat stage one, once again expressing a preference for either the original image or the symmetrical one.

The researchers found that the women who had been exposed to the slide show with more men in stage two ended up increasing their preference for male facial symmetry and decreasing their preference for female symmetry in stage three. Conversely, the women who had been exposed to the slide show with more women in stage two decreased their preference for male symmetry but increased their preference for female symmetry in stage three.

According to the study's authors, "women showed a greater increase in symmetry preference when judging the sex that was in the majority during the slide show than they did when judging the sex that was in the minority during the slide show." Based on this, they concluded that "women's evaluations of the attractiveness of both potential mates and potential competitors for mates are sensitive to cues of the sex ratio of the local population."

According to Watkins and his coauthors, women's shifting perception of attractiveness—not only for men but for other women as well—appeared to be an evolutionary adaptation that promotes "efficient allocation of mating effort." This adaptation reduces "within-sex competition" among women by decreasing their sensitivity to male looks and by increasing women's sensitivity to "the quality of potential competitors" at times when women are plentiful. The end result: Women are more likely to settle for less attractive mates when competition from other women is intense and more likely to hold out for attractive men when female competitors are fewer.

Some of the most intriguing new research on gender ratios takes Guttentag's theories beyond sex, love, and dating. Remember Ackerman, the MIT professor? In a 2012 article published in the *Journal of Personality and Social Psychology*, Ackerman, Vladas Griskevicius of University of Minnesota, and four other researchers raised an interesting question: Why do Columbus, Georgia, and Macon, Georgia—two cities a mere 100 miles apart, with a shared heritage and similar economies—have such drastically different spending habits? Columbus has one of the highest consumer debt rates in the country, while Macon has one of the lowest. Average consumer debt in Columbus is $3,479 per person higher than it is in Macon. Ackerman and his colleagues suspected the differences had something to do with sex ratios.

Macon has 0.78 single men for every single woman, while Columbus has 1.18 single men for every single woman. Ackerman's study does not explain why the two cities' sex ratios are so different, but there is one obvious explanation: Columbus is home to Fort Benning, the third-largest army base in the country. And though not part of the study, the oversupply of men in Columbus does appear to affect marriage and divorce in precisely the ways Guttentag anticipated. Compared to Macon, marriage rates in Columbus are much higher and divorce rates much lower. According to Census estimates for 2012, 36 percent of women age 20 to 34 are married in Columbus, versus just 19 percent in Macon. Additionally, 3 percent of the Columbus women in that age bracket are now divorced, versus 6 percent in Macon.

The big question Ackerman and his colleagues wanted to explore was whether sex ratios could influence spending and saving to the same extent they influence marriage and divorce. The answer was yes. Because men put more effort into dating when women are scarce—and also because "mating effort is associated with impulsivity"—Ackerman and his colleagues predicted that people living in cities with higher ratios of men to women would own more credit cards and carry more debt. They gathered sex-ratio statistics for 120 U.S. cities and compared them to regional financial data on credit cards and consumer debt. Turned out that men were indeed more financially impulsive when they had to compete: "A relative abundance of single men in America was related to both owning more credit cards and having a higher amount of debt."

Next, the researchers conducted psychological experiments in which they used slide shows to manipulate perceived sex ratios and to see if a male-heavy sex ratio would increase desire for immediate financial rewards. In the study, 205 men and women were shown head shots of young men and women, and told that the photo arrays—which varied from mostly male to mostly female—were representative of the local dating population. After being shown the photo arrays, the participants were then asked to choose between receiving a smaller sum of money today or a larger sum a month from now. For women, varying the sex ratio had no impact on their desire for immediate rewards. For the men, however, the sex-ratio effect was significant: The men were 40 percent more likely to choose immediate rewards when they perceived there to be more men rather than more women.

In a third experiment, study participants were asked to read fabricated news articles that described the local population as either having too many men or too many women. They were then asked how much money they would save that month as well as how much they would borrow on their credit cards. Once again, the results were consistent with the original thesis. The men intended to save 42 percent less and borrow 84 percent more when they believed there was a scarcity of women. Study participants were also asked how much men should spend on romantic purchases such as Valentine's Day gifts and engagement rings. When they thought the sex ratios skewed male, participants expected men to spend $6 more on Valentine's Day gifts and $368 more on engagement rings.

Ackerman and his colleagues noted how consistent these findings were with behavior observed in the animal world. "The fact that sex ratio has pronounced effects on economic outcomes is not surprising when one considers both theory in evolutionary biology and past research on operational sex ratios in numerous species." In other words, males invest more effort in finding and keeping a mate when females are in short supply.

Based on these findings, it might appear that having too many men can be a drain on the economy. After all, excessive credit card debt, low savings rates, and lavish spending on overpriced chocolates do not sound like a path to financial well-being. In reality, such negatives are more than offset by some big economic positives associated with high ratios of men to women. Ackerman's MIT colleague, economist Joshua Angrist, studied immigrant communities of the early-twentieth-century U.S. (remember, immigrants of that era were disproportionately male) and found that men earned about 10 percent more when sex ratios skewed male. Angrist's theory: Men are more successful at obtaining and retaining higher-paying jobs when they know they must make a strong financial commitment in order to secure a wife.

A 2007 paper by behavioral psychologists Thomas Pollet and Daniel Nettle of Newcastle University in the U.K. provided further evidence of women favoring wealthier men when men are in oversupply. Pollet and Nettle analyzed American Census data and concluded that in communities that were 52.5 percent male, lower-earning men were 2.3 times less likely to find a wife as compared to lower-earning men living in communities that were 50 percent male. Pollet and Nettle's finding is timely, as the non-college-educated dating pool in the U.S. is now 53 percent male. This may explain why marriage rates for non-college-educated women are higher than they are for non-college-educated men: Among those age 22 to 29 who are without a college degree, 30 percent of women were married in 2012, versus 22 percent of men, according to Census data.

Another timely study on the economic impact of lopsided gender ratios concluded that an oversupply of men has been an important driver behind one of the world's great economic success stories. The paper, "Sex Ratios, Entrepreneurship, and Economic Growth in the People's Republic of China," argued that China's draconian "one child" policy—a policy that left China with a massive oversupply of men thanks to sex selection, abortion, female infanticide, and foreign adoption of Chinese girls—has been an overlooked contributor to that nation's phenomenal GDP growth.

The China study's authors—Shang-Jin Wei, a finance professor at Columbia Business School, and Xiaobo Zhang, an economist with the International Food Policy Research Institute—understood their argument might sound far-fetched. "Robert M. Solow," they wrote, "the Nobel Prize winner for his pioneering work on the theory of economic growth, once said, 'Everything reminds Milton [Friedman] of the money supply. Well, everything reminds me of sex, but I keep it out of the paper.' Well, Solow might have missed something economically significant by not linking sex with economic growth."

Wei and Zhang's thesis was similar to Angrist's: In a society such as China's, with 122 men for every 100 women, women have more economic bargaining power when it comes to marriage, and that means young men and their parents must accumulate greater wealth in order to impress and secure a bride. (Chinese women are not shy about exploiting the lopsided conditions, as *The Los Angeles Times* reported in 2010. "I would rather cry in a BMW than smile on the back of my boyfriend's bicycle," the story quoted one Chinese bachelorette. A personal ad from another: "I'm 25 years old, looking for a boyfriend. I want you to have an apartment and a car. The apartment has to be built after 2000 and the car has to be better than a minivan.")

Wei and Zhang studied the economic choices made by families in the Chinese provinces with the highest ratios of men to women and compared them to those with the lowest. While sex ratios seemed to have no material impact on women or on parents with a girl child, they had a profound effect on men and on families with a boy: "[P]arents with a son and men respond to a rise in the sex ratio by engaging in more entrepreneurial activities, supplying more labor, and becoming more willing to take unpleasant or dangerous jobs, all in pursuit of a higher expected pay."

Based on their analysis, Wei and Zhang concluded that 20 percent of China's GDP growth from 2000 through 2005 was attributable to the oversupply of men and to the economic choices that men and parents of boys made in response. China's GDP grew at a 10 percent annual rate over those five years, and the economists predicted that China's sex-ratio-induced economic stimulus would expand over time, since the country's sex-ratio imbalance is projected to become worse over the next decade. The phenomenon that Wei and Zhang described is not unique to China. Later, I'll reveal the connections between the oversupply of men in Silicon Valley and the massive wealth creation now occurring in America's leading high-tech corridor.

Wei and Zhang's study may leave the impression that

only high ratios of men to women can increase economic productivity, but there is reason to believe that gender ratios lopsided in the other direction would have a similar effect if women were primary breadwinners. Consider the 2012 paper "Sex Ratio and Women's Career Choice: Does a Scarcity of Men Lead Women to Choose Briefcase Over Baby?" authored by Kristina Durante, a marketing professor in the College of Business at University of Texas at San Antonio, and four other scholars.

Durante and her coauthors took note of Guttentag and Secord's finding in *Too Many Women?* that the scarcity of men in medieval Europe—many men were lost to the Crusades—allowed women to achieve economic parity with men in the twelfth century. Based on that, Durante suspected that a shortage of men in some U.S. cities today would encourage women to pursue more lucrative careers. Her and her coauthors' theory: Women in communities with fewer men recognize the real possibility that they will not find a husband to help support them or their children.

The psychological experiments Durante and her coauthors crafted to test this hypothesis were similar to the ones used by Ackerman and Griskevicius (who was one of Durante's coauthors). The participants in Durante's study were women in their early twenties. The women were shown photo arrays—supposedly of singles on local dating websites. The slide shows were manipulated to make it seem as if there were either more men or more women. A second group of test subjects was asked to read news articles, purportedly from local newspapers, that described the local dating population as having either too many men or too many women. The women in both experiments were then asked questions about the importance to them of having a family versus having a career.

The results? Durante found a strong correlation between female perception that men were scarce and female desire for a lucrative career. Durante also concluded that women who identified themselves as being less attractive to men were even more likely to make career a priority when men were in short supply and when competition for men was intense. Sex ratios, Durante and her coauthors concluded, lead women "to seek lucrative careers when it will be difficult to secure a mate . . . [W]hether a woman chooses a briefcase or a baby—whether she invests heavily in a career or in starting a family—is related to the local mating ecology and the availability of mates." Given that many single, college-grad women are now grappling with a significant undersupply of men, Durante's finding may help explain why, according to a Pew Research report, millennial women have been closing the pay gap with men at an unexpectedly high rate.

In all of these psychological experiments, the men and women who adjusted their economic or romantic behavior did so after being made aware of lopsided sex ratios in their communities. Problem is, most college-bound high school students and most college-educated singles have no idea of the extent to which gender ratios have become unbalanced. Detmer, the Sarah Lawrence student, told me she thinks colleges should be obligated to put their gender ratios in bright, bold lettering on the cover of their brochures. The North Carolina high school guidance counselor quoted in the last chapter told me that she has never once had a parent or student ask about the 60:40 ratio at UNC Chapel Hill—despite the fact that this gender ratio is now a dominant feature of UNC social life. "It's not even on their radar," the guidance counselor told me.

It should be.

Chapter 4
Sex (Ratio) and the City

....

Why did the twelve New York City women cross the country to go on blind dates?

It sounded like a joke when I first read the news story. I was sure I knew the punch line, though, and it sounded as if the woman behind this cross-country dating adventure did too.

Lauren Kay is the 26-year-old founder of the online matchmaking site Dating Ring, and in 2014 she concocted a plan to fly a dozen single New York City women out to San Francisco for dates with Bay Area men. Yes, Kay's plan was a publicity stunt, but it was a really good one. The *San Jose Mercury News*, *Daily Mail of London*, *The Huffington Post*, Mediabistro, *The Denver Post*, *The Boston Globe*, and ABC News all covered the story. A writer for *New York* magazine even volunteered to participate and to write about her experience.

I wanted to find out whether Kay's idea was borne from the same demographic data I was exploring. Her comments to the *San Jose Mercury News* certainly had a statistical bent: "It is not that crazy to go to another city with better odds to look for someone special," she said. So I called up Kay and explained to her why I was so interested in her East Coast–meets–West Coast dating scheme. As it turned out, Kay had not been digging into demographic data, but the actual story behind how she hatched her plan proved far more interesting than any Census.gov spreadsheet.

Dating Ring is basically a hybrid between online dating and traditional matchmaking. Kay and other Dating Ring matchmakers interview new male and female members (sometimes in person but usually online), and then, with the help of proprietary computer algorithms, they match clients based on their personalities and dating preferences. Kay saw an opening for this kind of business model because traditional matchmaking is so expensive (with fees sometimes north of $10,000 a year) and because online dating can be time-consuming and sometimes fruitless. She noted that many of the online-dating boxes that people check off—height, race, hobbies, dog person or cat person, etc.—end up excluding people with whom they might just click. By adding a human touch to online dating algorithms, Kay aimed to get better results at a fraction of the price charged by full-service matchmakers.

Dating Ring opened for business in New York in 2013, and it wasn't long before Kay noticed a hitch in her sales data: There were three times more women signing up for Dating Ring than men. For singles over 30, it was five times more women than men. Kay knew she could never find dates for all these women, particularly those in their thirties and forties. She also knew that a spate of negative reviews on social media from disgruntled paying customers could be fatal for a start-up like hers.

Kay's solution was to cap the age of women members at 32. She chose 32 because that was the age at which the ratio of female to male sign-ups in New York surpassed 2 to 1. "It sounds horrible, but we weren't expecting to have so many more women than men," said Kay. "For the women above age 32, I didn't think we'd be able to set them up on dates."

Kay had discovered what older Manhattan women already knew—that single men in their thirties and forties who are both appealing and willing to date women their own age are a rare breed. "I call them 'unicorns,'" said Kay.

From a business perspective, Kay thought she was doing a good deed by declining to take the older women's money. The women being turned away thought otherwise. "I find it incredible," wrote one angry emailer, "that a progressive, interesting project like this would hew to such lame (and sexist) age standards. Be leaders, ladies."

Kay was mortified, but she stuck to her guns. "It was definitely not based on sexism—I was a women's studies major at Brown," she told me. "It was just the numbers."

Six months later, Dating Ring launched in San

Francisco, and Kay discovered that the numbers in the Bay Area were drastically different from those in New York. "In terms of the sign-ups, we were getting three men for every two women," said Kay. Thanks to Silicon Valley, the Bay Area has become a magnet for computer scientists, programmers, and engineers—fields that are disproportionately male. The oversupply of men was most pronounced for those 25 and under, but even for Bay Area singles in their thirties, Dating Ring's sign-up numbers still skewed slightly male. It was at this point that Kay hatched her idea for the cross-country dating event (which did yield one long-term relationship).

For Kay, the numbers had a personal impact too. Single and living in Manhattan at the time, she could not stop thinking about how much better the dating prospects were for women in the Bay Area. "That was one of the first times I started taking seriously how the choices I make now are going to affect me later on," she told me.

Not long after our interview, Kay moved to San Francisco. And within weeks of leaving New York behind, she began a serious relationship with a man she met at Y Combinator—a Mountain View, California, business-accelerator fund that also operates a mentorship program for young tech entrepreneurs.

"We're now moving in together and talking about marriage," Kay later told me in an email, recalling our earlier conversation about the abundance of men in Silicon Valley. "So, a bit fast, but I guess I took your advice to heart!"

♀♀♀♀

Is it possible that Lauren Kay would have found another Mr. Right had she stayed in New York? Of course it is. Nevertheless, it's hard to ignore the fact that Kay landed in a serious relationship after only three months in San Francisco, something that had not happened for her over the three years she lived in New York. What changed? It certainly wasn't Kay herself. What changed was her dating market. "People don't want to think of dating as a numbers game," she said, "but it is."

For women, the numbers game in New York is brutal. This chapter is the story of how lopsided gender ratios play out—how they affect dating behavior, and particularly how they affect men's willingness to commit. I've focused on New York City (and on the borough of Manhattan in particular) not because the city's oversupply of college-educated women is unique but because the stories are emblematic of the wider problem. That said, there are some distinctive demographic features of the Manhattan dating pool that do intensify the effect of the man deficit. So before hearing from Manhattan singles about dating life in the Big Apple, we first need to take a deeper dive into its dating demographics.

Believe it or not, based on Census data, Manhattan appears to be a good dating market for educated women—or at least a not-so-terrible one. Among those age 22 to 39, there are 26 percent more college-educated women than college-educated men in Manhattan, versus

27 percent more women than men nationally. On paper, Manhattan appears to be a better dating market for college-grad women than Chicago (29 percent more women than men), Raleigh (31 percent), and Minneapolis (30 percent).

In reality, however, Manhattan's and Minneapolis's respective marriage markets are night and day: 50 percent of educated Manhattan women age 30 to 39 have never been married, versus 32 percent in Minneapolis. (This Census data is tabulated by county—i.e., New York County for Manhattan, Hennepin County for Minneapolis, etc.) The problem with the data is that the Census Bureau does not ask people about sexual orientation in its decennial population counts, nor does it calculate such numbers for its yearly American Community Survey population estimates. For a city like New York, with a large gay and lesbian population, that omission complicates any attempt to accurately quantify the size and composition of the heterosexual dating pool.

Gender ratios within the gay and lesbian community have no impact, obviously, on whether the gay dating market or the lesbian dating market is in balance. They do, however, affect the heterosexual dating pool. According to Gary Gates, a scholar at UCLA's Williams Institute and a leading expert on LGBTQ demographics, gay men outnumber lesbian women by approximately two to one, with most surveys showing gay men accounting for about 2 to 3 percent of the male population and lesbians comprising about 1 to 1.5 percent of the female population. (Surveys show higher rates of gay and lesbian identification for people under age 30, Gates noted.)

The fact that there are more gay men than lesbian women—and consequently fewer straight men than straight women—has a relatively minor impact on the composition of the heterosexual dating pool nationally because gays and lesbians comprise a relatively small share of the overall population. In a city like New York, however, the impact is more significant. Contrary to popular belief, only a tiny sliver of the overall gay and lesbian population winds up clustering in LGBTQ-friendly cities such as New York, San Francisco, and Washington, D.C. Those who do relocate, however, are overwhelmingly white, male, and educated, according to Gates. "What we think of as gay enclaves are really rich, white, male gay enclaves," said Gates.

While the Census Bureau does not explicitly ask about sexual orientation, it does keep data on same-sex couples. And those numbers—all available on the Williams Institute website—demonstrate how Manhattan's gay and lesbian population skews an already lopsided heterosexual dating market. There are 16.7 same-sex couples per 1,000 households in Manhattan, versus only 5.5 per 1,000 nationwide. Given that the number of same-sex *female* couples per capita is no higher in Manhattan than nationwide, it appears that Manhattan's high rate of same-sex couples derives entirely from same-sex *male* couples. Indeed, 49 percent of same-sex couples are male nationally, whereas in Manhattan, 83 percent of same-sex couples are male. So Gates's gay-enclave theory—that these clusters are disproportionately male—appears valid. Extrapolating from the same-sex household data, Gates estimated that 9 to 12 percent of the male population in Manhattan is gay—closer to 9 percent for older men and 12 percent for younger ones.

Gates's analysis helps explain why the Manhattan dating market feels so much tougher on heterosexual women than the raw population count implies. If 11 percent of the under-40 male population in Manhattan is gay and 1.5 percent of the under-40 female population is lesbian, that means Manhattan's man deficit among heterosexual, marriage-age, college grads is not smaller than the national average, but larger.

Much larger.

Subtract the estimated gay and lesbian population from Manhattan's total population count, and you wind up with a hetero dating pool with 39 percent more college-educated women than men age 22 to 39—not 26 percent more. For the youngest college grads, the math is even gloomier (or even more wonderful, if you're a man): For college grads age 22 to 29, removing the gay and lesbian population from the numbers pushes the oversupply of women relative to men up from 39 percent to 54 percent—the equivalent of three women for every two men. And even these adjusted numbers may be too low, as gay men are more likely to be college educated than straight men, according to Gates.

One by-product of Manhattan's lopsided dating market is an intense pressure on Manhattan women to keep up appearances. "I was at a women's business event recently, and I couldn't get over how beautiful the women in the room were—women of all ages," said Maria Avgitidis, a Manhattan matchmaker and dating coach. Avgitidis contrasted Manhattan to Seattle, where an oversupply of men forces the men to shape up ("Seattle has some of the best-looking men in the country") and allows women to be more laid-back about their looks. "The first time I went to Seattle, I think I became the most beautiful woman in Seattle the moment I stepped off the plane," she kidded. Avgitidis is convinced that New York's reputation for beautiful women has less to do with genetics than with effort. That certainly rang true to Sarah Donovan, the single, 41-year-old journalist: She told me she's been known to spend thousands of dollars a year on her wardrobe—not to mention additional sums spent on hair highlights, bikini waxes, gym membership, eyebrow threading, facials, makeup, and all the other necessities for staying presentable to the opposite sex.

Just like on the college campuses, the scarcity of men in Manhattan keeps mental health professions busy too. "Of the women I see, I'd say that for eighty percent of them, their issues are related to singleness and fear of not finding someone," said Manhattan psychotherapist Kathleen Maher. "I had a patient yesterday who is forty-five. Her friends are paired off. She's constantly feeling alone. At this point she's more focused on just having satisfying friendships rather than a relationship."

"Sometimes they become preoccupied," Maher said of

single, female patients. "They are so anxious that they do things that kill off any hope of anything growing or happening. They are so primed for rejection that if the text message comes an hour later than they thought it should, they just can't tolerate it. They have to move on."

The flip side of women's dating angst is a huge pool of oversexed men. According to *TimeOut New York's* 2014 sex survey, New York men were one-third less likely than women to go without sex for long periods of time. And 39 percent of straight men in New York admitted to cheating, versus 29 percent of gay men. In national surveys, gay men report cheating much more often than straight men—presumably because straight men elsewhere have fewer opportunities.

You would think more men could be faithful to a woman like Carly Hansen.* Hansen is good company, she's drop-dead gorgeous, and she's a bit of a thrill-seeker too. "I'll be blunt," she told me. "I'm into kink."

Hansen, 32, grew up in Michigan and moved to New York City after college to work as a television production assistant. But after leading the New York single girl life for ten years, Hansen started to wonder whether it was time to move on. "My best girlfriends, they're all beautiful, wonderful women, and we all feel exasperated," she said. "Personally, I don't have the ties to the city that some of my girlfriends do. I'm kind of ready for the next step—especially after hearing the stats."

Manhattan's lopsided demographics helped Hansen make sense of her rocky love life. "I always assumed I just had bad luck in dating," she said. "Before moving to New York, I never would have considered an open relationship. But since I moved to New York, that's what all the guys seem to want."

One man broached the idea of an open relationship on their third date. "At least he was honest." Another took a more roundabout approach. "He was always voicing views against marriage or telling me about couples that had open marriages and how successful that was," Hansen said. "So I knew."

And it's not as if Hansen has a particularly rigid view of monogamy. Quite the opposite. "If a guy wasn't ready to commit because he wouldn't be able to have sexual experiences with other people, I'd be totally up for a conversation about bringing someone in occasionally," she said. "What I don't want is to be one of many."

Hansen did not have time for multiple men in her own love life, even if she were so inclined. Work and career took precedence. "Every guy I've dated has had a less stable career than me," she said—an observation that meshes with the scholarly research connecting gender ratios to work ethic. "It's almost like the guys in New York postpone growing up."

Now that Hansen knows the numbers, she said the behavior of New York men makes a bit more sense. "Why else would they be so obsessed with keeping their options open?" she said. The lopsided dating math also explained the weird sense of entitlement that New York men feel on online dating sites like OkCupid: "So many expect me to go out with them just because they sent me a message."

It put some of the worst offline behavior in context too. A few years ago, Hansen went out to dinner with her best friend, Zoe DeSantis,* and DeSantis's then-boyfriend. After dinner, the boyfriend brazenly felt up Hansen in the backseat of a taxicab that the three of them were sharing. "He thought we were going to have a threesome," said DeSantis—another one of my interview subjects— shaking her head in disgust.

"It's like a lot of men don't see us as people," DeSantis reflected. "I've had guys in New York admit to me that they expect women to be faithful to them but still be able to play the field themselves."

The oversupply of Manhattan women has so warped the sensibilities of men that matchmaker Avgitidis generally advises single women over 35 to leave the city. She recalled a conversation she had with a female reporter from CNN who had just moved to New York from Florida. "She came here thinking she'd meet men," said Avgitidis, founder of Agape Match. "I told her, 'Where did you get that idea?'"

For women over 35 who want to marry and have kids but don't want to leave New York, Avgitidis has an odd-sounding suggestion: "They should move to the suburbs." Avgitidis's argument is more qualitative than quantitative. She thinks a single man living in suburbia is more likely to be seeking a committed relationship than one living in Manhattan. For younger women, however, a statistical argument can also be made that suburbia is a hidden dating oasis. In suburban Westchester County, New York, for instance, there are 2 percent more single, college-educated men than women age 22 to 29, whereas Manhattan has 33 percent more such women than men. In suburban Lake County, Illinois, it's 12 percent more single women than men versus 34 percent more women than men in Chicago. Montgomery County, Maryland: 11 percent more single women than men, versus 26 percent more women than men in Washington, D.C.

Why are gender ratios less imbalanced in the suburbs? One explanation is men's greater willingness to commute to work: Nationally, 39 percent of male workers commute 30 minutes or more, versus 33 percent of female workers, according to Census data. (And, no, it's not because there are so many unemployed guys still living with their parents. Westchester County had an even greater oversupply of single men in 2005, pre-recession, than it does today.)

Obviously New York City does not turn every single, college-educated man into a sex addict. Even Hansen admitted to me that her preference for the edgy-artsy type probably had something to do with the high number of players she wound up dating. She actually emailed me after our breakfast interview to ask if I knew of any single guys I could set her up with. When I suggested a writer friend—a nice-looking guy, but one without an edgy bone in his body—Hansen dismissed him as too straitlaced.

That said, I don't blame women like Hansen for their own dating woes. Too many of the seemingly nice, normal guys I interviewed—especially those who had remained single into their thirties and forties—had dating histories similar to those of Hansen's and DeSantis's ex-boyfriends. My interviews with these men revealed the truth behind the contention of sociologists Uecker and Regnerus that men behave differently in different relationship markets. Lopsided gender ratios turn some nice guys into monsters.

Ben Waterman,* 37, morphed back into a nice guy five years ago. "I fell in love," he explained matter-of-factly. He met someone whom he felt was his intellectual equal. Someone whom he enjoyed spending time with outside the bedroom. Someone he wanted to raise children with. Someone he ended up marrying.

But throughout most of his twenties and early thirties, Waterman was not looking for any of those qualities in women he dated. He valued them mainly for their looks and their prowess in bed. He never had any intention of marrying these women. Of course, Waterman never told them that.

An average-looking guy who works for an advertising agency, Waterman moved to New York in his mid-twenties. He noticed right away that the kinds of women who had once been out of reach for him were suddenly flirting with him at bars and at parties. "I guess I thought it was because I was taking better care of myself," he said half-jokingly.

If not for the dramatic change in his dating market, Waterman might have married his college sweetheart and had kids young. But once he got a taste of Manhattan's sexual smorgasbord, he was not going back—at least not right away. "Suddenly you're fucking girls you could never fuck in high school," said Waterman. "If you're twenty-seven and you've been given something you've pined for for years, you're not going to just stop suddenly just because someone else thinks it's time to settle down."

The sheer number of women available to him encouraged him to think of his girlfriends as disposable. "I was much more cavalier about breaking up with women I was lukewarm on," he said. "At one point I was dating someone who was by far the most attractive woman—and by far the most sexually adventurous woman—I'd ever dated, and I broke up with her because I knew I could find someone just as wild but maybe a little smarter. A year or two before, it would have been inconceivable for me to even be with someone that hot and that sexy—never mind for *me* to break up with *her*."

The lopsided numbers also encouraged Waterman to think about infidelity more in terms of risk and reward than right and wrong. He recalled the summer when he and some acquaintances rented a weekend house in the Hamptons, a beach destination a couple of hours from New York. It wasn't long before Waterman started dating one of the women in the house. "It was one of those things where at the end of the night, it was understood that one of us would end up in the other's room," he said.

As fond as Waterman was of his summer fling, the

sheer number of women around him caused his eye to wander. "Whenever we went out that summer, I'd notice that me and all my [male] friends had several options wherever we were, and the girls from our house were desperately clinging to guys whom I didn't fear were a better option than me."

One night, Waterman brought home another woman from a bar and had sex with her within earshot of his summer girlfriend, who was sleeping in the next room. Needless to say, the girlfriend was not pleased. "But other than her being a little pissy the next day," Waterman said, "it took less than thirty-six hours for me to turn her out again. Even to me, that's astonishing. And just so you know, she didn't suffer from low self-esteem, and I'm not that amazing in bed. It was basically just, what was she going to do?"

Waterman's theory—that his girlfriend took him back simply because her own romantic options were limited—actually has some science behind it. So too does his observation that the oversupply of women made him more cavalier about breakups. Behavioral studies conducted by John Kim, a psychology professor at State University of New York at Geneseo, revealed that men value wives and girlfriends less when women are in oversupply and more when women are scarce: "A sex ratio with fewer members of the opposite sex conveys fewer mating opportunities and greater mating competition; accordingly, people become increasingly satisfied with their 'valued commodity' and feel closer to their partners as a result, which is consistent with both supply-and-demand principles," Kim wrote.

Kim also found that women are more likely to tolerate cheating by men when women are more numerous. He deemed this an evolutionary adaptation: Given the potential risk to mother and child should a mate who is a good parent and provider be lost, women are more likely to ignore "rivals who represent short-term sexual threats" if they believe doing so will maintain harmony and preserve the relationship. "This," wrote Kim, "is a less-than-ideal choice for women that is made necessary because of the unfavorable sex ratio in the local environment."

Waterman understood perfectly well that his local environment was what allowed him to behave as he did. Jason Hendriks* had not quite made that connection when I interviewed him. "Would I be less of an asshole if I didn't live in New York?" said the 34-year-old Hendriks, rephrasing my question. "I don't know."

A little pudgy and not exactly the world's sharpest dresser, Hendriks did not look or sound like a player when I met him. Eight years in Manhattan, however, had turned him into one. Unlike Waterman, Hendriks did not view his womanizing as some sort of phase. "It's not like I'm pining away for a wife and kids," he told me.

A self-described former computer geek, Hendriks took a job on Wall Street after grad school, and it was not long before he was a regular at a few different Upper East

Side wine bars where the women frequently outnumber the men two to one. (Census tract data indicates that among college grads 34 and under, there are in fact two women for every one man on Manhattan's Upper East Side.) Hendriks rationalized that he was making up for lost time after spending much of his college career holed up in a computer lab. He didn't feel bad about the one-night stands he'd promised to call but never did. Nor did he think twice about all the unreturned text messages from women he had kicked to the curb after only a week or two. The only time his conscience needled him was the time he got a phone call from his younger sister.

"She called me up and told me she was thinking about moving to New York," Hendriks said.

"No!" he told her. "The last thing you want to do is move to New York."

A recent law school grad who had taken a job in a small Midwestern city, Hendriks's sister was suddenly regretting her geographic choice. "I feel in New York I'd have a much better chance to meet the right guy and settle down," she told him.

"It's completely the opposite," he said. "I told her, 'The best place for you to be is a small town, a place where you don't have to put up with every guy acting like your brother.'"

That proved to be sound advice. Said Hendriks, "She wound up meeting a nice guy, and they're in a good relationship."

Of course, what Hendriks wanted for his sister was

not what he wanted for himself. "It's basically become a game to me," he said of his dating life.

The goal of this game was not to find a soul mate. The goal was to have as much sex with as many women as possible. At the time I interviewed him, Hendriks put his "number" at around two hundred. In order to rack up points, Hendriks exploited the man deficit to the hilt.

For instance, Hendriks believed that the shortage of men had intensified competition among New York women. It was an observation other single men shared with me as well. "They're always looking for a chance to tear each other down," Hendriks said. This happens in the animal world too, but male red phalaropes do not go out of their way to provoke infighting among the females. Hendriks does that exactly. He told me that one of his favorite first-date activities for winning a woman's trust—and for getting her into bed—was sitting with her at a sidewalk bar or café and partaking in some ill-natured people watching.

"So some girl walks by, and I'll say, 'Oh my god, did you see that trashy dress? What the hell is she thinking?'" he explained. "It creates rapport immediately—just by making fun of other girls in the city."

My friend Aimee Willis* is a 42-year-old single woman who probably knows the Manhattan dating market better than Warren Buffett knows the stock market. When I told her about Hendriks's first-date tactic, Willis was stunned—stunned not that the strategy worked but that a run-of-the-mill guy would know enough to try it. "Honestly, it's very fucked up but also true," said Willis, a wedding planner who pens a dating blog in her free time. "He's trying to relate with a woman the way a lot of them relate with each other—by putting other women down."

Another Hendriks observation that rang true for Willis was his contention that finding a woman who just wants to have sex is much easier at bars in Manhattan than it is elsewhere. "It's not every girl," Hendriks said, "but because of the sheer volume in New York, there are always going to be a bunch of girls at every bar who just want to hook up." Willis agreed with his assessment— much to her chagrin. "It makes life so much harder for the rest of us," she said.

Hendriks was not totally lacking in self-awareness. He knew his behavior was horrible, but it served his purpose. Because New York women were so desperate for some sort of relationship, he took chances with them that he never would have taken when he was younger. Asking a girl he had just met to go home with him had become a standard part of his playbook.

"When a girl plays hard to get, I just walk away," he said. "I'm simply not going to play that game, because I don't have to.

"The reality is that being forward can only help you. Either the girl is going to say, 'You're right, let's go home and fuck.' Or she's going to say, 'Fuck you.' And you know what? That's fine too because you're going to be wasting your time anyway if your intent is to get this girl to sleep with you. That's why, when you go out to a bar, you see a lot of New York guys being very forward—because that is ultimately going to be rewarded."

Waterman said something similar to me, though he couched it in a less boorish manner—one probably easier on the conscience.

"There was this one time I was making out with a girl at a friend's birthday party," Waterman recalled. "She was new to New York. This was our second or third date.

"At some point, she had said that she only has sex with people whom she was exclusive with. Well, it was getting hot and heavy, and we were talking about leaving, but I wanted to be a good guy. So I made her aware that while I did want to have sex with her, I wasn't ready for it to be a committed and exclusive thing.

"She got really angry at me. I looked at her and said, 'Listen, the only difference between me and every other man in this room is that I am telling you this now. Everyone else would tell you tomorrow morning.'"

The young woman's response? "She slapped me." Then she stormed off.

Years later, Waterman encountered this same woman at another party, and it was not long before she came over to say hello. "She told me I had been right," he said.

Much like Waterman, Hendriks viewed his Manhattan girlfriends as expendable: "As soon as it's too demanding or like a oh-honey-not-tonight sort of deal, guys are thinking, 'Well, this relationship is worth relatively little because it's so easy to find someone else.'" Hendriks knew how this sounded. "The conversations with my guy friends do get stupidly picky," he continued. "It's like, 'I like Sally but she's two inches shorter than my ideal height so I'm going to have to end things.' Or, 'She's ten blocks away, and it's not worth the hike.' It's insane. I guess it shows how spoiled we are."

Spoiled indeed. Helena Pearson,* a 39-year-old Manhattan marketing executive who grew up on a ranch in Montana, told me about one relationship that failed simply because the boyfriend did not like her routine of driving an hour upstate on Saturday mornings to go horseback riding.

"There probably are some women who are so desperate that they'd give up riding, but it's a big part of who I am," Pearson said. "What I want to know is where is the guy who says, 'Knock yourself out, babe—maybe I'll come with you next time.' Where is that guy?"

Perhaps the craziest Manhattan dating story I heard in this vein came from Jennifer Cooke,* a 40-year-old divorcée from Georgia whose husband left her not long after they moved to New York fifteen years ago. I met Cooke at a Manhattan cocktail party that could well have been an advertisement for this book. I counted a half dozen beautiful, ultra-successful, single women at this party versus only one unattached man.

When Cooke overheard me discussing my book research, she came over to share her favorite first-date horror story, one involving a drink-date with a Wall Street trader she had met online.

"I walked into the bar and saw him sitting alone—he

was the only guy sitting at a table. I went up to him and said, 'Hi, I'm Jen,'" said Cooke, a slender blond with a wry sense of humor.

"He looks up at me and says, 'Oh wow. You're not my body type *at all*,'" Cooke said. "Those are the first words out of his mouth!

"I gave him this strange look. I said, 'Oh really?'"

The guy's response: "Have you ever thought about breast augmentation?"

"Wow," she replied, "this is great because you just saved both of us a lot of time. But you're still going to buy me a drink."

One of the ways Hendriks rationalized his own bad behavior was convincing himself that many of the women were no more looking for love than he was. A lot of them, he claimed, were gold diggers. "Not long after I moved here, I remember saying hi to a girl at a bar, and the first thing out of her mouth was, 'What do you do?'" he recalled. "I was a little bit in shock—oh, you want me for my job. But at the same time, she's wearing an extremely low-cut shirt and I'm staring at her boobs. So the give and take was implied—I'm only interested in you physically, and you only want me for my money."

There is probably a small kernel of truth in what Hendriks described as "the give and take." Columbia University economics professor Lena Edlund studied the phenomenon of wealthy men marrying down economically and found that major cities do in fact attract disproportionate numbers of women who seek men with money and who relocate to locales where male salaries are higher and male wealth is more abundant. In a study published in 2005 by the *Scandinavian Journal of Economics*, Edlund found tangible evidence in European census data of women from lower socioeconomic strata relocating to wealthy urban areas to find men. The end result was an oversupply of women in many big cities.

"A surplus of women in cities may be a geographic manifestation of the general phenomenon of hypergyny, that is, women's marrying 'up,'" Edlund wrote. "So-called 'mail-order brides' provide graphic examples, but internal migration may be governed by similar forces . . . In fact, recent studies in molecular anthropology suggest that women have been more mobile geographically than men for a long time, and that this mobility may be linked to marriage." Of course, all this would have little statistical effect on the size of the man deficit if there were equal rates of gold digging by both sexes. Problem is, wealthy women are far less likely than wealthy men to marry down.

Eventually, an outflow of single women from Manhattan seems inevitable. Call it market forces. Call it nature abhorring a vacuum. At some point, college-educated women will stop flocking to New York City once they discover, much as Lauren Kay did, that the city's dating game is rigged against them. "Why are you still here?" was the question Manhattan matchmaker Avgitidis was constantly asking women who came to her for date coaching. It's probably an apt question for every Manhattan single woman who puts a very high priority on getting married.

Pearson, the Montana-born marketing executive, told me she's open to anything at this point—including leaving Manhattan and moving somewhere where she can get back in touch with her inner cowgirl. She travels frequently to rural Kentucky, and lately she's been thinking about relocating there permanently.

"I feel like I've tapped out my ambition here. I feel like I've done everything I want to do," Pearson said. "Now it's time to focus on other things. I grew up in a ranch town, I'm a big horse rider, and more and more, I want to be out of the city.

"I'm also sure there are a heck of a lot more men down there in horse country. For me, maybe that's the tipping point."

Chapter 5

The Woman Deficit

···

For Abby Evans,* leaving New York City was like grabbing a lifeline.

Evans had lived in New York since 2002, when she and her then-boyfriend, Brad, moved there after college. At that point in her life, men had never been much of a problem for Evans. "I think if you asked most people they'd say I'm kind, fairly extroverted, and reasonably attractive," said Evans, who was being modest.

In high school, Evans dated the star of the football team. In college, she hung with the other cool chicks. When she started dating Brad—a stereotypical math geek—the general reaction among friends was "What are *you* doing with *him*?"

"He's very handsome, but he was also very, very awkward socially," Evans said of Brad. "He had never even kissed a girl before he met me. I think he had obsessed about one other girl—in a very weird way—but never did anything about it."

Back in college, Evans was clearly the alpha in this relationship. But after she and Brad settled in New York, the dynamics began to shift. Evans really wanted to get married and start having kids: "My number one goal in life is to have a loving, happy marriage and have a family." But Brad, who had a high-paying job as a management consultant, was suddenly stiff-arming all marriage talk, even after he and Evans had been together for years.

"He got to New York and suddenly he was the most eligible bachelor around after years of not being in that position," said Evans. "He'd say, 'I love you so much, but I just don't feel ready. I've just never done this dating thing before—and by the way, I'm now in a really good position to do it.'

"It was heartbreaking for me. But finally, I said, 'That's it. You have till Labor Day to ask [me to marry you] or I'm moving out.'

"He didn't ask, so I moved out."

The breakup sent Evans into a tailspin. "I found myself thirty-two and totally single. I kind of panicked because I thought I was going to marry him." The two years that followed proved to be pure, unadulterated, New York dating hell for Evans. The guys she liked didn't want a serious relationship, and the guys who did want to date her were jerks. Things came to a head during a summer spent in the Hamptons. The Hamptons may

Central Islip Public Library
33 Hawthorne Avenue
Central Islip, NY 11722

have been the high point of Waterman's bachelor days, but for Evans, her own Hamptons summer was soul-crushing.

"It brings back such terrible memories," Evans said. "I always felt like I wasn't pretty enough or tall enough or popular enough—which were all emotions that I had not typically had in my life. I remember being at the Surf Lodge [a popular bar in Montauk, New York] and being surrounded by this sea of ridiculously beautiful women who were dressed to the nines. I was on a husband hunt, and I kept thinking, 'How am I ever going to meet someone when there are all these beautiful girls and all the guys are just looking to have a good time?'

"If guys can get away with one-night sorts of things, it becomes impossible to really engage with any of them."

Two years after her breakup with Brad, Evans's self-confidence was shot. "For most of my life I've been a happy and confident person," she said. "I felt a lot of that deteriorate in those last years of being in New York, desperately trying to meet somebody whom I could marry, literally before my clock ran out."

Contemplating a fresh start, Evans decided to visit some old friends in Aspen, Colorado—she had lived there for a summer in college—while also exploring the possibility of moving out to Aspen permanently. "I handed out some résumés," she said, "and the next thing you know I had a job offer and I was giving two weeks' notice in New York."

Dating-wise, Evans did not have terribly high hopes for Aspen. "There are only six thousand people total who live in Aspen, and I remember telling my mom, 'I'll probably never get married, because there aren't enough men, and I'm not going to marry a ski-lift operator.' But then again, it's not like I was having any luck in New York. The quantity might be greater in New York, but I wasn't meeting anybody."

What Evans did not realize was that she had chosen to relocate to one of the best small dating markets in the country for college-educated women. Because the skiing industry is so male-dominated, Pitkin County, where Aspen is located, actually has 22 percent more college-educated men than college-educated women among those 34 and under. "That is really interesting," Evans said after hearing the numbers for the first time. "Come to think of it, that first weekend I spent visiting, I was sitting at the hotel bar having a glass of wine when a guy sat down next to me and asked me out on a date. I remember thinking, 'Gee, that was easy.'"

So easy, in fact, that Evans wound up meeting her future husband, Darren—a handsome doctor with an outdoorsy streak—a mere eight days after moving to Aspen. She struck up a conversation with Darren at a local restaurant, and they've been a couple ever since, tying the knot in 2014. "I'm so happy," said Evans, now 36. "I just totally love him."

No, the Aspen Chamber of Commerce did not offer me complimentary skis or lift passes in exchange for sharing

Evans's story. Nor am I trying to push all the single ladies out of New York City. Obviously, most people are not going to choose where to live based entirely on dating prospects or on gender ratios.

What Evans's story does show is that dating demographics can vary significantly by region. Too few men in one area means there must be too many somewhere else—which is what Evans discovered when she traded in her high heels for hiking boots. If places like Manhattan have too many women, then there are going to be cities and towns like Aspen that do not have enough.

Up until now, I have divided the U.S. dating pool into two distinct markets—college educated and non-college educated—based on educated Americans' strong preference for mates with similar education levels. According to sociologists Schwartz and Mare, the odds of college graduates marrying each other "are higher today than in any other decade since 1940." While these two dating markets may operate separately, their demographics are inextricably linked. The U.S. is not China or India, where sex selection, abortion, foreign adoption of girls, and female infanticide have created a man-made woman shortage. In Western countries, total numbers of marriage-age men and marriage-age women are essentially equal, which means if there is an oversupply of women in the college-educated dating market, there has to be an undersupply of women in the non-college-educated one. As we shall see, the woman deficit in the working-class dating pool is real, even if the romantic challenges faced by blue-collar men do not receive nearly the attention nor sympathy heaped on the dating woes of urban, professional women.

Within the college-educated dating market, localized oversupplies of men are rarer than they are in the non-college-educated market. However, there are places such as Aspen where woman deficits do exist and also many others where gender ratios are more balanced. Nationally, there are 33 percent more college-grad women than college-grad men among those age 22 to 29, but there are 36 percent more such women than men in Illinois, 41 percent more in North Carolina, 48 percent more in Georgia, and 129 percent more in Alaska (yes, you read that correctly). If man deficits are above average in some states, they have to be below average in others.

So where are these more single-woman-friendly states? One of them is Evans's adopted home, Colorado. Ranked by the ratio of men to women among college grads age 22 to 29, the best dating markets for educated women in the U.S. are Wyoming, followed by Vermont, Maine, Washington State, Colorado, California, New Hampshire, Rhode Island, Connecticut, and South Dakota. Zoom out, and big-picture trends emerge. Regionally, the three best dating markets for educated women—and the three worst for educated men—are the Mountain West, the West Coast, and New England (particularly northern New England). For state-by-state sex ratios, see the table on pages 194–197.

None of these top-ten states actually has more college men than college women. Even in super-manly Wyoming, there are still 2.5 percent more college-grad women than men within the 22 to 29 age group. That said, a disproportionate number of the younger women in those ten states do seem to marry older men. Consequently, the number of *single* marriage-age, college-grad men does exceed the number of single college-grad women in Wyoming, Vermont, Maine, and South Dakota. Wyoming actually has 41 percent more single college-grad men than women in the 22 to 29 age group. Maine has 17 percent more.

Like Wyoming, Alaska is another western state known for having lots of men, which makes Alaska's absence from the top-10 list worthy of a closer look. Alaska's leading industries—fishing and oil-and-gas production—are male-dominated. Because so many more men than women move to Alaska for work, the state's overall population skews male. According to the Census Bureau, Alaska had 11 percent more men than women as of 2013—which adds up to a lot of lonely bachelors. There's even a magazine marketed to women, *Susie's AlaskaMen*, which features profiles of single Alaskan men looking to meet that special somebody.

Yet despite Alaska's well-earned reputation for having an overabundance of men, the state actually has the biggest man deficit in the country within the *college-educated* dating pool. In the 22 to 29 age bracket, Alaska has 2.3 college-grad women for every one college-grad man, according to Census data. Thankfully for Alaska's educated women, the man deficit does not play out there the same way it does in other states: 37 percent of under-30, college-grad women are married in Alaska, versus 31 percent nationally. Alaskans, it seems, are much more open-minded about education when it comes to choosing their mates. Sarah Palin's husband, Todd, did not graduate from college, nor did former Alaska U.S. senator Mark Begich—whose wife, Deborah, did.

The man deficit may be a nonissue for educated Alaskans, but it does pose problems for non-Alaskan women who move up there seeking educated men. It can even stymie a seasoned dating professional like Richard Gosse, a San Francisco–based organizer of upscale singles events and also the chairman of the Society of Single Professionals. Gosse used to hold a national singles convention every year, and he was always looking for new ways to attract more men. "Every year I would have too many women and not enough men," he told me. "So one year I decided to go to the one city in America where I knew there are too many single men."

The city was Anchorage. "It was terrible," Gosse recalled. "I'm having professional women flying from around the United States to Anchorage to find an Alaskan bachelor to marry. You can guess what happened." I did: There were too many educated women and not nearly enough educated men. "It was one of the worst singles conventions I ever did," Gosse said.

If Gosse were still holding national singles conventions today, the first city on his list would be San Jose— which, along with the rest of Silicon Valley, he considers the best dating market in the country for single women. "San Jose is a single woman's paradise in terms of finding a quality man," said Gosse. "Not only are the men plentiful, but they tend to be the cream of the crop—the best educated, the most intelligent, and the highest-income men in the country. If you can't find a good man in Silicon Valley, you're in trouble."

He's got a point. Among those with a college degree, Santa Clara County has 45,736 men and 40,889 women age 22 to 29, according to 2012 Census estimates. In the 30 to 39 age bracket, it's 78,427 men and 76,321 women. And because the marriage rate for Silicon Valley women is much higher than it is for men (78 percent of women in their thirties are married, versus only 70 percent of the men), the gender ratios for *single* men and women are considerably more lopsided than for the overall population. Among those age 20 to 29, there are 38 percent more single men than women in Santa Clara County; for those 30 to 39, it's 48 percent more single men than women. (For county-by-county sex ratios, see table on pages 198–205.)

The dating market feels even more lopsided than that for men employed in the technology sector, simply because so many men work in offices where women are few and far between. According to Census data, 76 percent of computer and engineering jobs in Santa Clara County are held by men, which translates to three men for every one woman.

"For an engineer in Silicon Valley, your day is something like this," said 26-year-old tech entrepreneur Henry Pasternack.* "You get on a bus in the morning, and there are no women. You work in a department in which there are twenty men and one woman. You go to lunch, and there are some women—maybe they work in sales and marketing—but they're all talking either to each other or to the CEO . . . For guys in tech, there's definitely a sense of hopelessness when it comes to women."

For employers, however—all engaged in a never-ending race to build the hottest new app or device—this hopelessness can be a good thing. Fewer women means less competition for the time and attention of their male programmers and engineers. "Countless VCs, pundits, founder helpers, xfounder VCs, and most anybody else involved in the Valley/SF start-up scene will ask you, 'When are you moving out here? This is where it is happening,'" wrote Tom Summit, a Boston-based tech blogger and a recruiter with Genero Search Group. "Step right up, come one, come all. They want you, they need you, and they will own your butt. Because what they don't tell you is that you will have nothing else to occupy your attention and keep you from working eighty hours a week cranking code with your nose in a computer screen. Why? Because there are no women to distract you from your tasks."

For all that today's young male college grads may be ridiculed for being happy couch potatoes (to borrow a line from Hanna Rosin), the lazy-guy stereotype does not fit the young men of Silicon Valley. Not even close. Silicon Valley's woman deficit has helped spawn a 24/7 work culture that exists in no other U.S. high-tech hub. Pasternack said he was working 110 hours a week at his start-up before his health deteriorated and his doctor urged him to cool it. At Apple, even Sunday nights are work nights, according to Nitin Ganatra, Apple's former director of engineering for iOS apps. "There's this fire hose of emails that are just going out at 2:45 in the morning, and there are VPs or executive VPs who are scrambling to get answers," Ganatra said in an iMore.com podcast. "And that was just week after week, month after month."

Santa Clara County boasts the highest household median income in the country. I am not suggesting that median incomes there would be merely average were it not for the shortage of women. It does appear, however, that the same phenomenon Wei and Zhang observed for China—a scarcity of women producing higher levels of entrepreneurism and industriousness among men—has also super-charged wealth creation in America's high-tech mecca.

"It's sort of like prison," Pasternack said in semi-jest. "In prison, guys have nothing else to do other than be hypercompetitive with each other about building the biggest muscles. In tech, with no women around, guys get hypercompetitive about building the biggest bank accounts." So hypercompetitive that, according to the research firm WealthEngine, there are now 91,000 millionaires living in San Jose, the equivalent of 10 percent of the city's total population.

Colin Hodge, the 30-year-old founder of the dating app Down, had no doubt that the shortage of women in the Bay Area fuels the competitive streaks of Silicon Valley entrepreneurs like himself. "A lot of my dating success in

San Francisco has come as a result of running a successful start-up," said Hodge. "Women are more likely to see you as a prize rather than just another guy who blends into the background. It raises your dating value.

"Now, if that's your *only* motivation career-wise, you've got problems. But I would say that for a lot of entrepreneurs, part of the dream of blowing up and having a successful start-up involves the social benefits that come with it."

This extra motivation is missing in locales where women are more plentiful. Hodge mentioned a programmer buddy who relocated to New York City for work. "He and I were talking about New York, and he actually said he had to rein it in after his first year," Hodge said. "The distractions—the opportunities to meet new women and go out on dates—were overwhelming.

"It's not like he was going to get fired or anything, but he said if you're not careful, it can be a de-motivating factor."

For the women of the Bay Area, the local gender ratios actually allow for a healthier lifestyle simply because a disproportionate number of men are not holding out for Porn Star Barbies. "These are genuinely good guys who have a more romantic notion of courtship and marriage," said Amy Andersen, founder of Linx Dating, a Menlo Park–based matchmaking service that works primarily with Silicon Valley men. "They're just not well versed when it comes to playing the field. They're good guys. They don't want to be jerks."

Amber Kelleher-Andrews, another Bay Area match-maker, went so far as to attribute the stereotypical difference in appearance between southern California and northern California women—L.A. women resembling starlets, San Francisco women frumpy hipsters—to the conduct of men in their respective dating pools. In L.A., men like to play the field, whereas in the Bay Area, men are more inclined to settle down, Kelleher-Andrews said. (Among college grads age 22 to 29, there are 24 percent more women than men in Los Angeles, versus 5 percent more men than women in San Francisco and 12 percent more men than women in Santa Clara County.) "There's so much competition for men in Los Angeles that the women spend a lot of time on themselves, on looking good and dressing right," said Kelleher-Andrews, CEO of Kelleher International. "In L.A., a man can go out to lunch with a woman whom he thinks is beautiful, and all of a sudden another woman walks by who is more beautiful, and then there's a woman in the corner who is even more beautiful.

"Here [in the Bay Area], what's really interesting is that you can go out to lunch and you won't notice anybody. Then all of a sudden a beautiful woman walks through the door. The odds are she's from southern California."

Avgitidis shared a similar observation from one of her business trips to Seattle. (About half of Avgitidis's business is Greek American matchmaking, and Seattle has a sizable Greek population.) She recalled walking into a semi-upscale bar after a meeting, wearing a designer dress and heels. Avgitidis looked around the bar and noticed that most of the other women were dressed as if they'd just returned from a day hike. No makeup, casual shoes, etc. "I started talking to one woman, and she couldn't believe that I wasn't married," Avgitidis said. "There are just so many men in Seattle, me not being married didn't make sense to her."

There are more men than women in Seattle overall, but the perception that educated men there are in oversupply is only partly true. Among those 22 to 29, Seattle actually has 12 percent more college-educated women than men, though among singles there are slightly more men than women. Of course, any oversupply of men—even a slight one—still makes Seattle a fantastic dating market for college-educated women when compared to most of the country.

As I'll show later, there are only a handful of well-populated areas in the country where college-grad men outnumber college-grad women. If you want to find actual woman deficits (and not just not-so-bad man deficits), you need to look beyond the white-collar bastions and zoom in demographically on America's blue-collar dating market. When you examine the overall U.S. population—not just the college educated—the biggest woman deficits are found in those areas that offer the best job opportunities for blue-collar men.

The states with the highest ratios of all men to all women are, from highest to lowest: Alaska, Wyoming, North Dakota, Nevada, and Utah. The first three are all big oil-and-gas states; as I said, it is not uncommon for young roughnecks to be earning $60,000 a year or more. Utah has oil and gas too, along with military bases and mining operations (not to mention countless ski resorts) that help drive up the male head count.

If Nevada seems like the outlier on the list, that's only because the gender demographics of the gaming and entertainment industries go unnoticed by the throngs of tipsy tourists clogging Las Vegas's casinos and nightclubs. Nevada actually has 10 percent more men than women age 20 to 29. The upshot: Despite its Sodom-and-Gomorrah-like reputation, Nevada has above-average marriage rates for women age 20 to 29. In Nevada, 37 percent of college-educated women and 31 percent of non-college-educated women are married, versus 31 and 30 percent nationally.

Like Alaska, North Dakota is another state with an overabundance of men overall but an extreme shortage of men in the college-educated dating pool. And much like Alaska, North Dakota's college man deficit—the state has 70 percent more college-educated women than men age 22 to 29—has little negative impact on the marriage prospects of educated women. Among those age 22 to 29, 42 percent of college-grad women in North Dakota are married, versus 31 percent nationally.

Alaska and North Dakota also ranked numbers 1 and 2, respectively, in Gallup's 2014 U.S. Standard of Living Index survey, thanks in large part to all the good-paying jobs provided by oil and gas. I'm confident there is a connection between the high marriage rates of educated women in those states and the greater availability of high-paying, blue-collar jobs for men. Despite studies to the contrary, educated women are willing to marry non-college-educated men so long as those men earn a good, stable income.

Problem is, due to the fifty-year decline in U.S. manufacturing and the rising job insecurity within the working class, blue-collar men with stable incomes are in shorter supply these days. As a result, white-collar women are less likely to seek them out. Most non-college-educated men are thus stuck in a dating market that is almost as tough for them as the Manhattan dating market is for women like Carly Hansen. In blue-collar communities, more women than men are heading off to college and not returning home, creating a woman deficit for men left behind. According to the Census Bureau, there are 12,715,896 non-college-educated men in the U.S. age 22 to 29 versus 11,261,287 such women. And the gender gap is even wider among those who are single—9,415,116 men versus 7,088,033 women.

Talk to dating professionals in working-class communities, and the impact of this woman deficit becomes clear. Dutchess County, a largely working-class area in upstate New York, has 32 percent more single, non-college-educated men than women among those age 22 to 39. This woman deficit posed problems for local speed-dating organizer Debby DiGregorio of Pre-Dating Speed Dating of Hudson Valley. Whereas matchmakers in Manhattan struggle to find eligible men, the challenge for DiGregorio has been finding enough women to attend her events. "Me, I've got men coming out of my ears," DiGregorio told me. "Just tonight I had to turn away seven men from an event . . . I never have enough women, especially in the younger groups."

The dating woes of non-college-educated men extend beyond raw numbers. Just as scholarly studies predict, working-class men must work harder to attract a wife when women are scarce: Among fully employed, non-college-educated men age 25 to 30, the men who were married earned 20 percent more than those who were not, according to 2012 U.S. Census Bureau data.

There is also anecdotal evidence that some non-college-educated women have responded to the woman deficit much the same way educated men have responded to the man deficit. Researchers David and Amber Lapp of the Institute for American Values, a conservative think tank, interviewed 75 working-class young adults in Ohio for their Love and Marriage in Middle America Project. One of the Lapps's findings was a pattern of infidelity—among the women. For example, the Lapps told the story of Tanya, a young woman who left her husband and two kids for her next-door neighbor. "I love him, but I'm not in love with him," Tanya said of her ex-husband. "I love him as a friend, as the father, but I don't feel that connection as I used to . . . like, not at all."

More than half of the thirty-eight men interviewed in the Lapps's study reported that they had been cheated on or that they suspected being cheated on. Ricky, one of the

Lapps's male interview subjects, sounded just as resigned to infidelity by his girlfriends as Hansen did when discussing her New York City boyfriends.

"I kinda expect it even though it's shitty to expect it," said Ricky. "Even if the girl isn't that type of person, I do expect it. I mean, I don't think she's going to. But in the back of my mind, I kind of say, 'Hey, she could.'"

Chapter 6

Mormons and Jews

···

What about values?

It was the question that always came up whenever I'd discuss various theories on marriage rates or the hookup culture with my friends and family.

"Couldn't it just be that times have changed?" people asked.

Times have changed, and that is a good thing—especially the fading away of cruel taboos that stigmatized women who engaged in premarital sex or who bore children out of wedlock. But much like Guttentag, I cannot accept the idea that times change for no reason. "The values question," as I called it, seemed to assume that sexual mores loosen inexorably from rigid to liberal. In reality, these values ebb and flow, often in conjunction with prevailing sex ratios.

Of course, tales of scarce men and sexual permissiveness in ancient Sparta are not going to convince everyone, so I began to explore the gender demographics of modern-day religion. I wanted to show that godfearing folks steeped in old-fashioned values are just as susceptible to the effects of shifting sex ratios as cosmopolitan 20-somethings who frequent Upper East Side wine bars. Eventually I hit pay dirt.

One of my web searches turned up a study from Trinity College's American Religious Identification Survey (ARIS) on the gender demographics of Mormons. According to the ARIS study, there are now 150 Mormon women for every 100 Mormon men in the state of Utah—a 50 percent oversupply of women. I had never read anything about a Mormon marriage crisis, but if these numbers were correct, I knew there had to be one. So on a lark, I emailed my friend Cynthia Bowman,* a devout Mormon who grew up in Salt Lake City and returns there often, and asked her whether Mormon sex ratios are as lopsided as the ARIS study claimed.

Yes, she told me, the ratios are lopsided. And yes, Mormon men take full advantage. "They wait for the next, more perfect woman," grumbled Bowman, a veterinarian in San Diego. Premarital sex remains taboo for Mormons, but the shortage of Mormon men was pushing some women over the brink. "There might actually be a more promiscuous dating culture than there otherwise would be in the Mormon culture because of this gap," Bowman said. "I do know women who have had sex with Mormon men because they have thought this might increase their chances of getting the guy to marry them."

Months later, still neck-deep in Mormon research, I got lucky a second time. I received an email from a hedge fund manager—a friend of a friend—who wanted to talk to me about a job. I called back to thank him for thinking of me but explained that I was busy writing a book. He asked what the book was about. I wound up telling him about the Mormon marriage crisis.

"Wow," he said, "that sounds a lot like the Shidduch Crisis."

The Shidduch Crisis? I had never heard of it, but the Shidduch Crisis turned out to be a marriage crisis among Orthodox Jews remarkably similar to the marriage crisis afflicting Mormons. On paper, Mormons and Orthodox Jews appear to have about as much in common as physicists and fishing-boat captains. Orthodox Jews tend to live in tight-knit, insular communities. Their wardrobes are often as ultra-conservative as their beliefs—dark suits for the men and rather dowdy, skin-concealing blouses and skirts for the women. Orthodox Jews are intensely devout, and many consider daily study of Torah and Talmud to be their ultimate calling. Mormons, on the other hand, believe salvation comes not from studying sacred texts but from living happy, moral lives in ways that conform to their teachings—and from sharing those teachings with others. And while Mormons may be socially conservative, that does not mean they can't strive to be fit and stylish (and cheerful!) too.

Yet as dissimilar as these two religious communities may appear from the outside, both suffer from nearly identical marriage crises that are testing not only their faiths but social norms as well. "You have no idea how big a problem this is," said Tristen Ure Hunt, founder of the Mormon Matchmaker, a Salt Lake City dating agency.

Hunt, a 35-year-old who only recently got married herself (to a man ten years her junior), told me she has three times more single women than single men in her matchmaking database. She shared stories of devout Mormon women who wound up marrying outside the religion—officially known as the Church of Jesus Christ of Latter Day Saints—simply because they had no other options. She has ten friends—"all good LDS girls!"—who gave up on finding a husband and decided to have children on their own. Said Hunt, "My heartstrings are pulled daily."

Two thousand miles away in New York City, Lisa Elefant knows exactly what Hunt is feeling. "I don't sleep at night anymore," said Elefant, a *shadchan*—or Jewish matchmaker—affiliated with the Ohr Naava: Women's Torah Center in the Sheepshead Bay section of Brooklyn. "My own sister is thirty-seven, educated, accomplished, attractive, and single. I told her to freeze her eggs." Secular-style dating is rare in the Orthodox community in which Elefant lives. Most marriages are loosely arranged—"guided" is probably a better word—by matchmakers such as Elefant. The *shadchan*'s job has been made exceedingly difficult, she said, by a mysterious increase in the number of unmarried women within the Orthodox community. When Elefant attended Jewish high school thirty years ago, "there were maybe three girls that didn't get married by the time they were twenty or twenty-one," she said. "Today, if you look at the girls who graduated five years ago, there are probably thirty girls who are not yet married. Overall, there are thousands of unmarried girls in their late twenties. It's total chaos."

For Orthodox Jewish women, as for Mormon ones, getting married and having children is more than a simple lifestyle choice. Marriage and motherhood are essentially spiritual obligations, which is why the Orthodox marriage crisis is so hotly debated and why it has earned its own moniker. *Shidduch* is the Hebrew word for a marriage match, and thus Orthodox Jews (including the more assimilated Modern Orthodox) now refer to the excess supply of unmarried women in their communities as the Shidduch Crisis.

Mormon and Orthodox Jewish leaders alike fear that their respective marriage crises reflect some failure to instill proper values in young people. Perhaps young people are too self-absorbed? Maybe the men are just too picky? Or maybe it's the women who are holding out for the Mormon or Jewish George Clooney and need to be more willing to settle? In fact, the root causes of both the Shidduch Crisis and the Mormon marriage crisis have little to do with culture or religion. The true culprit in both cases is demographics. The fact is that there are more marriage-age women than men both in the Orthodox

Jewish community and in the Utah LDS church. And just as I predicted, lopsided gender ratios affect conservative religious communities in much the same way they affect secular ones.

At first glance, the state of Utah—60 percent Mormon and home of the LDS church—looks like the absolute wrong place to study the man deficit. Like several other western states, Utah actually has more men than women. In fact, Utah's ratio of men to women across all age groups is the fifth highest in the nation. But lurking beneath the Census data is a demographic anomaly that makes Utah a textbook example of how shifting gender ratios alter behavior.

The LDS church actually has one of the most lopsided gender ratios of any religion in the United States. According to the ARIS study, there are three Mormon women for every two Mormon men within the state of Utah. And sure enough, the undersupply of Mormon men is affecting this traditional religious community— one scripturally committed to early marriage and parenthood—in some rather perverse ways. Mormon women find themselves at the mercy of an entitled group of Mormon men who are delaying marriage in response to their seemingly endless array of dating options. Most Mormons still marry by their early twenties, but, according to the state's Office of Vital Records and Statistics, Utah's marriage rate declined by 19 percent between 2000 and 2008—more than the national average. Singles in their thirties and forties—once "unheard of" among Mormons—are now the fastest growing segment of the Mormon dating pool, according to a *Huffington Post* article on the Mormon marriage crisis.

"There are so many options for the men, it's no wonder it's hard for them to settle down," said Deena Cox, a single, 34-year-old office manager who lives in Salt Lake City.

One fact that quickly becomes apparent when studying the demographics of religious groups is that it is almost always the women who are most devout. Across all faiths, women are less likely than men to leave organized religion. Statistically speaking, an atheist meeting may be one of the best places for single women to meet available men. According to the Pew Research Center, 67 percent of self-described atheists are men. And Trinity College's 2008 ARIS survey found that men comprised 60 percent of those Americans with no religious affiliation.

Due to men's generally higher rates of apostasy, it makes sense that the modern LDS church, like most religions, would have slightly more women than men. The Utah LDS church was in fact 52 percent female as recently as 1990. Since 1990, however, the Mormon gender gap in Utah has widened dramatically—from a gender ratio of 52:48 female to male in 1990 to 60:40 female to male in 2008, according to a study coauthored by ARIS researchers Rick Phillips, Ryan Cragun, and Barry Kosmin. In other words, the LDS church in Utah now has 50 percent more women than men—or three women for every two men. (Outside of Utah, the gender ratio is more balanced:

A Pew Research survey found that there are 27 percent more Mormon women than men nationwide.)

The sex ratio is especially lopsided among Mormon singles. Many individual LDS churches—known as "wards"—are organized by marital status, with families attending different Sunday services than single people. Parley's Seventh, one of Salt Lake City's singles wards, had 429 women on its rolls in 2013 versus only 264 men, according to an article in the *Salt Lake Tribune* newspaper. The dating math is most daunting for older single women. A 2014 *New York Times* article on Mormon life in Utah reported that there are now ten single Mormon women over age 40 for every four over-40 single Mormon men. Census numbers for Utah County—80 percent Mormon, home to the city of Provo and Brigham Young University—showed something similar: Among those age 40 to 49, Utah County had seven single women for every four single men.

Kelly Blake* is painfully aware of the horrible odds. A single Mormon in her late thirties, Blake is a reporter for a Salt Lake City television station. When Blake attends singles events for Mormons, she said there are often two women for every one man. As a result, Blake rarely meets suitable men in these settings and often winds up spending most of her time chatting with other women. "I'll go on a [Mormon] singles cruise and come away with no dates but all these incredible new girlfriends," Blake told me.

Like Cox, Blake said Mormon men are more likely to hold out for the perfect wife because their dating pool is so vast. "I call it the paradox of choice," said Blake. "For men, there are so many choices that choices are not made." And once Mormon men are ready to settle down, their single, female contemporaries may no longer fit the profile of the ideal Mormon wife. "The dream for the Mormon man is to get married and have six kids," she said. "As he ages, his dream never changes. But when you're a thirty-seven-year-old woman, you've already aged out of that dream."

So why are there so many more Mormon women than Mormon men? The simple answer is that over the past twenty-five years, Utah men have been quitting the LDS church in unusually large numbers. ARIS's Cragun, a sociology professor at the University of Tampa who is ex-LDS himself, said the growing exodus of men from the LDS church is an unexpected by-product of the growing importance of the mission in Mormon life.

Contrary to popular belief, the majority of Mormon men do not go on missions, which typically entail a mix of community service and proselytizing. Historically, only 30 to 40 percent of Mormon men have served the two-year missions. Some Mormon men prefer to get on with their educations or their careers, whereas others simply cannot afford missions' cost. Serving a mission can run $400 or $500 per month in travel and living expenses, and the bills are footed not by the LDS church but by the missionaries themselves, or by their families.

Fifty years ago, there were few negative consequences for men who did not serve missions. "I actually had a stake president growing up who didn't serve a mission," said Cragun. (In the LDS church, the stake president is the lay equivalent of a Catholic bishop.) "In the 1950s or 1960s, it was more elective. You could get away with not serving a mission."

That began to change in the 1970s and '80s, when LDS leaders began pushing for all able-bodied young men to serve missions. Today, serving a mission is essentially a prerequisite for leadership positions within the church. Not serving can be a source of shame for men, especially for Mormons in Utah. (Outside of Utah, there is less social pressure to serve missions. This may explain why the gender ratio among non-Utah Mormons is less lopsided.)

Mormon men who never served a mission tend to avoid the subject. "In the church context, people are going to ask, 'Why didn't you serve?'" said Cragun. "'What was wrong with you? What's your disability?' If you don't have a disability, you are less righteous for not having served. You can't say, 'I didn't want to.' That's an awful thing to say. You have to have wanted to. It's built into the culture. It's expected.

"So if you choose not to serve a mission, the question becomes, Why would you stick around [the church] at all? Why would you face that social stigma for the rest of your life? It makes no sense."

The timing of the mission compounds the problem. Mormon men are being asked to serve missions at precisely the time in their lives—late teens and early twenties—when sociologists say men are most susceptible to dropping out of organized religion. Cragun believed the dropout problem among men is the real reason why, in

2012, the LDS church lowered the age at which Mormon men can start serving missions from 19 to 18: "I think they were losing too many men who would go off to college or get a job before they turned nineteen and then realize they didn't want to stop and serve a mission."

Lowering the mission age seems to be having the intended effect: Between 2012 and 2014, the number of Mormons serving missions increased from 58,000 a year to 83,000, according to the LDS website. If this trend continues, the lowered mission age should reduce the Mormon gender gap and ease the Mormon marriage crisis over time. Of course, that is cold comfort for today's single Mormon women, as the loss of men from the church has affected not only the supply of men, but men's conduct too.

There is ample evidence that Mormon men are delaying marriage. News articles on this topic tend to be filled with tales of Mormon women who desperately want to marry but cannot find a good Mormon man. Gender ratios are never cited as the reason why men are in no rush to wed. The *Salt Lake Tribune* published an article in 2011 (headline: "Why Young LDS Men Are Pushing Back Marriage"), which blamed the marriage crisis on Facebook ("After we've learned everything about each other on Facebook, what do we talk about on the first date?") as well as a "modern nonchalance" about marriage. LDS leader Richard Scott was quoted chastising young men to grow up: "If you are a young man of appropriate age and are not married, don't waste time in idle pursuits. Get on with life and focus on getting married. Don't just coast through this period of life."

The *Tribune* story cited a survey of Mormon college students in which men expressed a belief that age 30 is now the right age to get married. The finding was unexpected, given that most Utah Mormons marry by their early twenties. In the same article, Brigham Young University professor David Dollahite complained of a "market mentality" among men at the LDS-dominated campus. When it came to dating, BYU men seemed paralyzed by indecision. "The young men think, 'I am dating a 9.7, but if I wait, maybe I could get a 9.9,'" Dollahite told the *Tribune*.

Based on enrollment figures, BYU men should not be so picky. In 2013, the gender ratio among BYU undergrads was actually 54:46 *male* to *female*. With 17 percent more men than women on campus, it is the BYU women who should be the choosy ones. But because social life at BYU is so atypical compared to most colleges, the campus-wide enrollment figures do not reflect the university's actual dating market. Yes, there are more male undergrads overall, but BYU's freshman class in 2013 was actually 62 percent female—or three women for every two men. The change in the mission age probably exaggerated the freshman gender gap for 2013, but according to data available on the BYU website, BYU's freshman class has been majority female every year since at least 1997. In 1997, for instance, BYU's freshman class was 59 percent women.

What's going on? Hannah Wheelwright helped

unravel the mystery for me. A 2014 BYU grad, Wheelwright explained that it is quite common for BYU women to marry male classmates while still in school and that a significant number of the newlywed women wind up dropping out of college. Consequently, the gender ratio among the *single* students at BYU more closely resembles the gender ratio of the freshman class than it does that of the overall student body.

Single BYU men are keenly aware of the lopsided numbers, said Wheelwright, who is a leader of Ordain Women, a feminist organization seeking the appointment of women to the LDS priesthood. "In the dating market, the men have all the power," Wheelwright said. "Men have all these options, and the women spend hours getting ready for dates because their eternal salvation and exultation depends on marrying a righteous, priesthood-holding man."

Even BYU men who are eager to marry are not shy about pressing their statistical advantage. "A Mormon man at BYU will go up to the woman who is the most popular, the most in shape, and then tell her, 'I have prayed and I have received a revelation and God wants you to marry me,'" said Wheelwright. "It sounds like Mormon folklore, but I know women it's happened to. It's just another way men try to use leverage."

Sex is another such way. To be sure, the Mormon dating scene at BYU—or in Utah in general—will never be confused with the bacchanalia of Sarah Lawrence or of Manhattan's Upper East Side. As I said, premarital sex is still taboo for Mormons. Yet, just as Bowman suggested, the undersupply of men does seem to be loosening Mormon sexual mores. "At BYU, a lot of Mormons my age don't consider oral sex to be sex," said Wheelwright.

One way to quantify the increase in sexual activity in Utah is by examining statistics for sexually transmitted diseases. On a per capita basis, chlamydia infections among Utah women increased 88 percent between 2001 and 2011, a growth rate 37 percentage points higher than the national average, according to the U.S. Centers for Disease Control. Then there's Duck Beach. Commonly known as "Mormon spring break," Duck Beach started out as an innocent social event for Mormon singles on the North Carolina shore. But in recent years Duck Beach has morphed—at least according to a 2012 *GQ* article—into "a four-day weekend of debauchery full of sex, booze, and wild experimentation." *GQ* reported things had gotten so out of hand at Duck Beach that LDS leaders were now advising local stake presidents to discourage their singles from attending.

From a sociological perspective, Guttentag probably would have loved Mormon Utah. In *Too Many Women?*, she and Secord argued that women are more likely to be treated as sex objects whenever men are scarce. That is precisely what Mormon women now experience. "Women's bodies are up for debate," Wheelwright complained. Mormon men have become much more demanding about women's looks, which in turn has made women obsessed with standing out from the competition. One consequence: A culture of plastic surgery has taken root among Mormon women. "I have seen more outrageous boob jobs and facial plastic surgery in Utah than almost anywhere in the country—especially among Mormon women," said Bowman. "They may claim chastity as a virtue overall, but that's not stopping anyone from getting a set of double-Ds."

Mormons rushing to get boob jobs may sound far-fetched, but Bowman's assertion is supported by the leading consumer review site for cosmetic surgery, RealSelf.com. According to a 2011 RealSelf study, Salt Lake City residents did more searches for breast implants on the RealSelf website than residents of any other city. Moreover, a 2007 *Forbes* story labeled Salt Lake City "America's Vainest City," with four plastic surgeons for every 100,000 people, which was 2.5 times the national average. Salt Lake City residents also spent inordinate sums on beauty products—$2.2 million in 2006 on hair coloring and $6.9 million on cosmetics and skin care products, according to *Forbes*. By comparison, Oklahoma City, a city with a slightly larger population, spent $172,000 and $594,000, respectively.

In this cosmetic arms race, the big guns are Botox, liposuction, and breast augmentation. "There are so many attractive girls here, the guys get choosy," explained Dr. Kimball Crofts, a Salt Lake City plastic surgeon. (He speaks from experience. Mormon himself, Crofts did not marry till his forties.) Crofts said his office has college-age women coming in for Botox injections. And the day

I interviewed him, Crofts had just finished a consultation with an attractive woman in her twenties seeking a breast augmentation. "Cute girl. Pretty breasts, but smaller," he told me. "She says to me, 'I don't want them too big, but my boyfriend would really like them bigger. He's dated a lot of girls with big breasts. I've seen all the pictures, and I'm the only one who's smaller.'"

Hunt, the Mormon matchmaker, believes there is a clear connection between the hypercompetitive dating market and the plastic surgery obsession and body-image issues affecting some Mormon women. "It's hard for some women to keep their self-esteem at a high place when you feel the competition and you're not getting any dates," said Hunt. "I used to joke that there are more eating disorders at BYU because the competition is so fierce. Fact is, there are some really good-looking, attractive LDS people."

Hunt told a story of a male matchmaking client who balked at being set up with a beautiful blond who could not have weighed much more than 100 pounds. "He's looking at her photo telling me, 'Well, her booty is kind of big,'" Hunt said. "I'm like, 'Are you kidding me? You have no hair on your head and you're complaining about her booty? Get a grip!'

"Of course, I didn't actually say that, because the reality is that Mormon men do have endless options."

My favorite interviewee on the Mormon marriage crisis was Steven Rinehart, a thoughtful, 38-year-old patent attorney who lives in Salt Lake City. When I contacted Rinehart, he had just gotten married. But two years earlier Rinehart had been featured prominently in that aforementioned *Huffington Post* article. According to the article, the then-single Rinehart had all the makings of a great catch—fit, attractive, successful, and religiously observant (he told the reporter he had never had sex or consumed alcohol). "I just can't find the right one," he said at the time. "I have to take seriously that there is some sort of internal psychological resistance to settling down. I don't think there is, but other people do."

Intrigued by his comments, I called up Rinehart and asked him whether he thought the marital indecision of Mormon men like himself might be linked to an oversupply of Mormon women. "Well, the numbers are lopsided, and something does happen with the men—they become more selective as they get older," Rinehart said, adding that some men even refer to the singles wards as "meat markets." Rinehart observed a connection between the growing Mormon singles scene and increased rates of premarital sex and alcohol consumption among Mormons. "It's a changing culture," Rinehart offered. When I suggested to him that perhaps the culture had changed because of the demographics—and not the other way around—he paused.

"I hadn't thought about it the way you have," Rinehart said. "You may be right."

Rinehart had many insights into why it had taken him so long to get married, but the explanation that really piqued my interest involved his frustration with the left-wing leanings of some of the Mormon women he had dated. "I was having a lot more friction with women over political topics than I used to," Rinehart said. He contended that as single Mormon women entered their late twenties and thirties, their political and religious views became more liberal. Quite conservative himself, Rinehart could not picture being married to someone whose worldviews clashed so profoundly with his own.

"Here's one example," he said. "I remember going out to dinner with a woman in 2005 right after Hurricane Katrina. As we were pulling out of the parking lot, I commented that it had been two or three weeks since Hurricane Katrina, and the flags were still flying at half-staff. The flags are only supposed to be flying at half-staff for five days. She interpreted the comment about the flags as being racist. She said, 'Well, that's a very racist thing to say—that you don't think people should be expressing sympathy for Hurricane Katrina victims, who are predominantly African American.'"

This "friction" with older single women extended to religious doctrine too. "There seemed to be an increasing number of women who were upset that the church didn't share their points of view on women's rights or feminism," Rinehart said. "Their points of view on those issues seemed to be changing from what typified single women when I was in my twenties. One woman spent dinner telling me all the reasons why the Mormon church was sexist and how she could barely stand it.

"And this was someone who is active in the Mormon church every Sunday."

Rinehart's observations fit neatly into Guttentag's theory that feminist movements are energized by over-supplies of women. Men take advantage of imbalanced gender ratios, and women fight back by seeking to reduce their social, political, and economic dependence on men. Cragun, the University of Tampa sociology professor, saw the connection. So too did Wheelwright, one of the young leaders of the Ordain Women movement. "I think it's a contributing factor," Wheelwright said. "It all relates to the immense pressure women feel to be as marriageable as they can—to be the ideal, perfect Mormon woman—which is affected not only by gender ratios but by the religious socialization they receive."

For Wheelwright, it was hard to separate what she perceived as ingrained gender bias in Mormon doctrine from the demographic impact of too many women in the LDS community. She believed both contribute to a "toxic perfectionism" that afflicts Mormon women. "There's a powerlessness women experience in the church," she said. "The only thing you can control is your body, so you get plastic surgery or you try to have more kids."

This is one reason why Wheelwright believed allowing women a leadership role in the teaching of LDS gospel is so important. As things stand now, getting married and having kids is the Mormon woman's primary responsibility within the LDS faith, she said. The lopsided gender ratios feed preexisting disillusionment among Mormon women by making their core duty—getting married—difficult, degrading, or even impossible. Said

Wheelwright, "In a religion where women are already unnecessary to the essential structure of the church, having a gender imbalance where you have too many women just compounds that effect."

Before I interviewed Orthodox Jewish matchmaker Lisa Elefant about the Shidduch Crisis, I emailed her the *Huffington Post* article about the marriage crisis affecting Mormons. What was going on in Utah sounded an awful lot like what was happening in Orthodox Jewish communities, and I was curious whether Elefant would see the similarities. "It sounded very familiar," Elefant remarked after reading the story. "This is what happens. There are these eligible guys, and you're wondering, 'What is going on? Why won't he get married?'"

As with the Mormon marriage crisis, the Shidduch Crisis has become a source of enormous heartache for Orthodox Jews, especially older single women and their parents. (Among Orthodox Jews, "older" often starts at 21.) The Letters to the Editor section of *The 5 Towns Jewish Times*, a weekly newspaper for the Orthodox community in suburban New York, has become a receptacle for Shidduch Crisis–related angst and sadness. "An absolute tragedy," is how one mother described the situation. It is "what we as a family and I as the mother of a 27-year-old 'older single girl' go through every moment of my life, every breathing second of every day. And believe me, sometimes it hurts to do just that—i.e., to breathe."

Single Orthodox women tend to cope better than their Jewish mothers. Three young women's playful Shidduch Crisis musical parody—titled "Make Me Babies" and sung to the tune of Carly Rae Jepsen's hit "Call Me Maybe"—has garnered 35,000 views on YouTube. (The lyrics: "You're still taking your time . . . And I'll be nineteen soon . . . My mommy cries every day . . . Did you see my résumé? . . . Hey! This is crazy! 'Cause you and I met twelve days ago . . . and we're not engaged yet.")

Others joke that the Shidduch Crisis has turned supposedly devout Jewish men into womanizers. "Funny how I found a guy right away when I started meeting guys who aren't Orthodox, and there was no pressure for sex early on as there is with supposedly *frum* [pious] men," one woman wrote on the Orthodox humor site FrumSatire.net.

The similarities between the Mormon and Orthodox marriage crises go beyond shared sorrow. When Wheelwright first mentioned how "women's bodies are up for debate" in the Mormon world, my first thought was New Yorker Jennifer Cooke's first date with the guy who wanted her to get a boob job. My second was an interview I had conducted with Dr. Michael Salamon, a Long Island, New York, psychologist who works with the Orthodox community and who wrote a book on the Shidduch Crisis. Salamon had told me a story about a frantic mother who called his office, pleading that he meet with her daughter and the young rabbinical student whom the daughter was set to marry.

"I squeeze them in on a Friday morning, they come in, and they're both dressed already for Shabbat," Salamon said. "He's wearing a shiny new black suit, and he's got these fancy cuff links that they all get when they get engaged—it's like a disco ball, the room shines up because of the cuff links. She comes in with him, conservatively dressed, a nice young woman, maybe nineteen years old."

Salamon asked the couple what the problem was.

"I would like my wife to have breast reduction surgery," the young man replied.

Salamon was confused. He turned to the young woman. "Well, that's what he wants," she said, nodding.

"I look at her," Salamon recalled, "and it's clear she doesn't need breast reduction surgery. She's not out of proportion in any way. She's a nice-looking woman. So I asked him: 'Why?'"

The man's answer: "I don't want anybody else to look at her."

The statistical explanation for why Orthodox men are in short supply is different from the one for the shortage of Mormon men. Orthodox men are not abandoning their faith in large numbers and leaving Orthodox women behind. According to a recent Pew Research study, only 2 percent of Orthodox Jews are married to non-Jews, and the attrition rate from the Orthodox movement to the more mainstream Reform or Conservative branches of Judaism has actually been declining.

The imbalance in the Orthodox marriage market boils down to a demographic quirk, the same one that caused the overall U.S. marriage market to become lopsided after World War II. The Orthodox community has an extremely high birth rate, and a high birth rate means there will be more 18-year-olds than 19-year-olds, more 19-year-olds than 20-year-olds, and so on and so on. Couple the increasing number of children born every year with the traditional age gap at marriage—the typical marriage age for Orthodox Jews is 19 for women and 22 for men, according to Salamon—and you wind up with a marriage market with more 19-year-old women than 22-year-old men.

How many more? According to Pew Research, the average number of children born to American Orthodox Jews is 4.1. This high birth rate (for the general public, it's 2.2) adds up to 4 percent annual population growth within the Orthodox community, according to Joshua Comenetz, chief of the U.S. Census Bureau's Geographic Studies Branch and an expert on the demographics of Orthodox Jews. "By comparison, the overall U.S. population grows about 1 percent a year," Comenetz said.

There is no U.S. Census data on religion—Comenetz's research on Orthodox Jews dates back to his days as a professor at University of Florida. But based on his academic research, Comenetz contended that each one-year age cohort in the Orthodox community has approximately 4 percent more members than the one preceding it. What this means is that for every 100 22-year-old men in the

Orthodox dating pool, there are 112 19-year-old women—12 percent more women than men.

The impact of this gender gap extends beyond statistics. As in the secular world, a 12 percent gender gap in the marriage market affects more than 12 percent of the women because lopsided sex ratios incentivize men to delay marriage and to play the field. Given that the supply of younger women increases every year, men who wait to settle down until age 28 often wind up marrying women who are five or six years their juniors, instead of two or three. The bottom line: According to a 2013 article in the Jewish weekly *Ami Magazine*, there are now 3,000 unmarried Orthodox women between the ages of 25 and 40 in the New York City metro area and another 500 over 40. That's a huge number when you consider that New York's Yeshivish Orthodox—the segment of the Orthodox community most affected by the Shidduch Crisis—has a total population of 97,000, according to the Jewish Community Study of New York published by the UJA-Federation of New York in 2012.

That is the Shidduch Crisis in a nutshell. Unfortunately, relatively few Orthodox Jews realize that the Shidduch Crisis boils down to a math problem. Most explanations for the Shidduch Crisis blame cultural influences for causing men to delay marriage. "Those of us who've tossed and turned with this, we don't necessarily believe that there are more girls than boys," said Elefant. "We believe God created everybody, and God created a match for everybody."

As Elefant saw things, a 22-year-old man inherently has more dating options than a 19-year-old woman, because he can date down age-wise. "The guys act like kids in a candy store," Elefant said. Of course, if there were gender-ratio balance among all the age cohorts, single 22-year-old men would not have more choices than single 19-year-old women because most of the age-19-to-22 women would already be married to older men—thus shrinking 22-year-old men's dating pool.

With Mormons, there is no scientific way to settle the culture-versus-demographics argument. You cannot create a social experiment with 50 heterosexual single women and 50 heterosexual single men, tell them they can only marry other study participants, and then observe whether outside cultural influences cause young Mormon men to play the field and delay marriage, even when the gender ratio is even. In the Orthodox Jewish community, however, there is a natural control group—one that does make it possible to settle the culture-versus-demographics debate with near certainty. That control group is a sect of Orthodox Judaism known as Hasidic Jews.

The core beliefs of Hasidic Jews differ from those of other Orthodox Jews in nuanced but spiritually significant ways. Hasidic Jews believe each daily act of religious observance creates a personal, perhaps mystical, connection with God. In contrast, their counterparts in the Yeshivish (sometimes referred to as Lithuanian) branch of Orthodox Judaism emphasize the study of Torah and Talmud as the primary means of growing closer to God.

While their religious practices may differ, the two groups are still quite similar culturally. Both Yeshivish and Hasidic Jews are extremely pious and socially conservative. They live in tight-knit communities. They are known for having large families. And both groups use matchmakers to pair their young men and women for marriage. There is, however, one major cultural difference between the two groups: Hasidic men marry women their own age, whereas Yeshivish men typically marry women a few years their junior.

"In the Hasidic world, it would be very weird for a man to marry a woman two years younger than him," said Alexander Rapaport, a 36-year-old Hasidic father of six and the executive director of Masbia, a kosher soup kitchen in Brooklyn. Rapaport is a few months older than his wife, and that's typical for Hasidic husbands and wives. Sometimes it's the women who are a bit older. Sometimes it's the men.

When I asked Rapaport about the Shidduch Crisis, he seemed perplexed. "I've heard of it," he said, "but I'm not sure I understand what it's all about."

In fact, there is no Shidduch Crisis in the Hasidic community. "When I mention the term to Hasidim, they don't know what I'm talking about," said Samuel Heilman, a professor of sociology and Jewish studies at City University of New York and an expert on Hasidic Jews.

Another academic, Hershey Friedman of Brooklyn College, reached the same conclusion, but from a different vantage point. When Friedman is not writing about Jewish culture or teaching finance at Brooklyn College, he volunteers as a matchmaker for Saw You at Sinai, an Orthodox dating service that combines traditional matchmaking with some of the tools of online dating. Friedman is not Hasidic himself, but he's intimately familiar with the Hasidic community because he lives in Borough Park, a Brooklyn neighborhood considered the epicenter of American Hasidic life. "The girls have it made in the Hasidic world," Friedman said. "They're the ones in demand." Friedman's explanation for the absence of a Shidduch Crisis among Hasidic Jews is that there are more Hasidic boys than girls—a perception that I suspect is inaccurate but nonetheless reflects how different the marriage market is for Hasidic versus non-Hasidic Orthodox Jews.

The seeming immunity of Hasidic Jews to the Shidduch Crisis has not been lost on Yeshivish rabbis. Moshe Pogrow, a rabbi in Queens, New York, was one of the first to identify the high birth rate and the age gap at marriage as the root causes of the Shidduch Crisis. Pogrow's analysis was spot-on, but his market-based solution proved controversial. Pogrow's organization, the North American Shidduch Initiative, offered to pay thousands of dollars (money provided by women and their families) to matchmakers who could find husbands for older single women. Many in the community found the idea degrading—particularly since the size of the payments rose with the age of the women.

In 2012, a dozen American and Israeli Orthodox rabbis signed letters urging young men and their parents to begin their matchmaking process earlier than age 22 or 23. The rabbis noted that their community "finds itself in an increasingly difficult situation," with "thousands" of single Jewish women struggling to find husbands. "[I]t has become clear that the primary cause of this is that [men] generally marry girls who are a number of years younger," read one of the letters. "Since the population increases every year and there are more girls entering *shidduchim* than boys, many girls are left unmarried. Clearly, the way to remedy this terrible situation is to reduce the age disparity in *shidduchim*. Many [Hasidic] communities who do not have age disparities in *shidduchim* are not facing this tragic situation of numerous unmarried girls."

The suggestion that the true origin of the Shidduch Crisis lies in demographics has not sat well with those who staked their reputations on alternative explanations. "This fancy cocktail of demography, sociology, mathematics, and mythology is really nothing more than a Ponzi scheme," American Rabbi Chananya Weissman wrote in *The Jerusalem Post*. "More men will not magically appear if we manipulate who marries whom and try to buy some time."

Weissman runs an organization called End The Madness, which aims to reform the Orthodox matchmaking system. Weissman places much of the blame for the Shidduch Crisis on the women themselves. As he wrote on TheYeshivaWorld.com website, women are too focused on "non-Halachic externalities" (i.e., attributes not valued by Jewish law or tradition) when evaluating prospective husbands: "I would posit that feminism and un-Jewish values have had a devastating effect on the *shidduch* world . . . The same women who are supposedly just desperate to get married, who want nothing more than to meet a nice guy who doesn't drool all over himself, categorically reject the vast majority of men they come across without batting an eyelash—and then say the problem is there aren't any good guys out there."

Weissman's solution is for Orthodox Jews to rely less on matchmakers and more on singles events where young Orthodox men and women can mingle and get to know each other in more natural settings. Of course, there's plenty of natural interaction between college-educated men and women in Manhattan, and that hasn't solved the too-many-women problem in the secular world.

The reality is that most of the cultural explanations for the Shidduch Crisis advocated by folks like Weissman confuse symptoms with causes. One letter-writer to *The 5 Towns Jewish Times* blamed the boys for being coddled and lazy: "[T]he caliber of the girls and women of today is far superior to that of their male counterparts. The women are goal-oriented, put-together, articulate, and polished—while their male counterparts are lost souls. Many have no direction. Many have no drive." Of course, this is exactly what the social science on gender ratios predicts: Whichever gender is in the majority tends to be more industrious.

Perhaps the most controversial—and definitely the most misogynistic—explanation for the Shidduch Crisis was offered up by Yitta Halberstam, coauthor of the best-selling Small Miracles series of books. Halberstam's 2012 column in *The Jewish Press* started out innocently enough. "This is the harsh truth," she wrote. "The mothers of 'good boys' are bombarded with *shidduch* suggestions on a daily basis—a veritable barrage of résumés either flooding their fax machines or pouring out of their email inboxes—while those with similarly 'top' daughters sit with pinched faces anxiously waiting for the phone to ring. The disparity is bare, bold-faced, and veritably heartbreaking . . . [B]oys are constantly being courted and pursued, while the best girls' résumés barely elicit a modicum of interest."

Halberstam knew all this because her own son was going through the matchmaking process: "I feel a little sad each time the fax machine cranks out yet another résumé for my son. I know full well that there are *fantastic* girls out there who are his equals—perhaps even his superiors—who are NOT receiving comparable treatment. They are neither being hounded nor pursued half as vigorously as he, and they are denied the latitude of choices that he receives every day. I ache for their mothers, who repeatedly call the *shadchanim* [matchmakers] who never call back, but are visibly more responsive if you are the mother of a boy. Inwardly, I rail against the unfairness of it all."

This is where Halberstam went off the rails. She went on to describe attending a community event where single women were introduced to mothers of single men—and being "jolted" by the subpar looks of the girls. "Yes," she wrote, "spiritual beauty makes a woman's eyes glow and casts a luminous sheen over her face; there is no beauty like a pure soul. Makeup, however, goes a long way in both correcting facial flaws and accentuating one's assets, and if my cursory inspection was indeed accurate (and I apologize if the girls used such natural makeup that I simply couldn't *tell*), barely any of these girls seemed to have made a huge effort to deck themselves out."

In other words, the real reason these young women were still unmarried was because they were homely. Halberstam then doubled down on heartlessness, suggesting that a visit to the plastic surgeon might be in order for some of these plain Janes: "Mothers, this is my plea to you: There is no reason in today's day and age with the panoply of cosmetic and surgical procedures available, why any girl can't be transformed into a swan. Borrow the money if you have to; it's an investment in your daughter's future, her *life*."

The uproar over Halberstam's column was predictable. "The most universally offensive article about *shidduchim* that the world has ever seen" is how rabbi and Jewish blogger Eliyahu Fink described it.

"I can't help but make the comparison to the currently popular 'Hunger Games' phenomena where the characters are forced to fight to the death simply because some crazy woman decided so," wrote blogger Deena Sasoon on the FrumSatire.net website. "Ms. Halberstam, is this your version called the 'Shidduch Games: Lose Yourself to Find a Man'?"

Of the 648 mostly shocked and outraged comments posted to *The Jewish Press* website, one in particular stood out: "Dear Mrs. Halberstam, I am also a Jewish mother," it began. "But I no longer share your joyful anticipation of walking my child down to the *chuppa* [the Jewish wedding canopy]. She died last year, of anorexia.

"It all began six years ago, when, at the age of 21, a *shadchan* who professed to be as well-meaning as you do suggested that she lose a few pounds (she was a size 6 at the time) in order to make herself more 'marketable' (that is the term she used then). What followed was a nightmare for her, me, and our whole family that I can only hope you will never know from. If you have a modicum of *rachmunus* [pity] in your Jewish *neshama* [soul] I beg you to retract this article and apologize for your deeply, dangerously misguided advice. I am crying now as I write this and think of what my daughter had to suffer because of exactly the type of things that you have written here, and I am just so afraid for all the other impressionable young girls who will read your words and reach the same end. This is not a joke, and it is not funny at all. You could literally be killing people by making these suggestions and perpetuating the ethos that underlies them."

This was no overreaction. Anorexia has in fact become a quiet scourge of the Orthodox Jewish community. A report on the National Eating Disorders Association (NEDA) website described the intense pressure that single Orthodox women feel to stay thin during the matchmaking process. NEDA cited a study by eating disorder specialist Dr. Ira Sacker, who found that one in nineteen girls in one Orthodox community had been diagnosed with an eating disorder. That diagnosis rate was 50 percent higher than that of the general U.S. population.

Orthodox blogs are filled with stories of Jewish men who refuse to consider marrying women whose dress sizes are larger than a 6 or an 8. "When people discuss *shidduchim*, which is THE most important thing that controls [an Orthodox] girl's life, if she's more than a 6, she's considered 2nd rate," one young woman wrote on the now defunct frumteens.com website. "I have friends who are constantly being told by their parents that they better 'slim down' or else!"

Writing in *The 5 Towns Jewish Times*, nutritionist Pamela Moritz recounted her own failed attempt to schedule a lecture on "how to eat healthy without dieting" at an Orthodox girls' high school.

"We can't have you speak here," the principal told her. "The girls need to lose weight or they'll never get a *shidduch*."

"Excuse me?" Moritz replied.

"You and I know that it isn't right," the principal said, "but these girls want to get married and they know that if they're a size 14 or bigger, they'll never get a *shidduch*. You can't tell them not to diet."

Because the Orthodox marriage market is so challenging for women, there is pressure not only on young women to remain thin but also on parents to hide any eating disorders should their daughters develop one. "For arranged marriages among the ultra-Orthodox, the first question matchmakers ask is about physical appearance, including weight and the mother's weight, which feeds the message that thinner brides are more desirable," the Associated Press reported in 2010. "Parents, match-makers and potential mates want a svelte bride, but may shun a woman who divulged she has an eating disorder because of the stigma of mental illness." The end result is that Orthodox families are disinclined to acknowledge eating disorders, often seeking help only "when a girl is on the verge of hospitalization."

One cultural by-product of the Shidduch Crisis that has not been hushed up is the ever-larger dowries that Orthodox brides and their families are now expected to pay for the privilege of getting married. These dow-ries are typically financial promises made by the bride's parents to help support the young family for the three or four or however-long-it-takes years that their future son-in-law may spend studying Torah and Talmud at a Jewish seminary. The fact that these dowries keep increas-ing demonstrates both the market power men possess as well as the desperation felt by young women and their par-ents. "It was never like this before," said Salomon. "There was always a dowry, but it was pillowcases and things of that nature—not $50,000."

Salomon noted that the practice of brides' families pay-ing five- and six-figure dowries has begun to leach from the traditional Orthodox community into the smaller but more assimilated Modern Orthodox one. Indeed, the Summer 2013 issue of *Jewish Action*, the official magazine of the Modern Orthodox umbrella organization Orthodox Union, included an essay by Rabbi Lawrence Kelemen, a well-known Jewish scholar and lecturer. Kelemen told the story of his own attempt to arrange a marriage for his daughter: "When I contacted the head of a prestigious American yeshiva [an Orthodox Jewish seminary] to ask if he might have a *shidduch* for my daughter, he asked me 'what level boy' I was interested in. Unsure what he meant, I asked for clarification. 'Top boys go for $100,000 a year, but we also have boys for $70,000 a year and even $50,000 a year.' He said that if I was ready to make the commitment, he could begin making recommendations immediately."

The Orthodox Union's executive vice president, Rabbi Steven Weil, told me he believed a backlash to the increasingly outlandish dowries was brewing. "You don't marry for money," Weil said. "This is not our religion."

Weil is right, of course. It is not his religion. It is his religion's demographics.

Chapter 7
Game Theory

....

By now, a few of you are probably thinking: Jon, there is no way gender ratios can explain *every* change occurring in today's dating market!

My response: You're absolutely right!

Of course there are dating market quirks completely unrelated to gender ratios—and others that are only tangentially related. I've long wondered, for instance, why the single women who are the most panicked about their marriage prospects seem to be some of the most attractive, likable women I know. I've also wondered why so many divorced men become more desirable in their forties than they had ever been in their late twenties—despite now having less hair, bigger guts, and, in some cases, incomes shrunk by alimony and child support.

But just because these curiosities cannot be explained

by gender ratios alone does not mean they can't be understood scientifically. As a result, my research veered off on a few tangents. This chapter—in which I explore how mathematics, probability, psychology, and race affect specific dating and marriage outcomes—is the end result.

Let's start with a question lots of people probably *think* they know the answer to: Why is the marriage market for a college-educated, 40-year-old woman worse than it is for a comparable 27-year-old woman? Based on demographics, the 27-year-old should actually have a harder time finding a guy, since she graduated into a more lopsided dating market. The 40-year-old completed college at a time when there were 17 percent more women than men graduating from college; the 27-year-old graduated when the gender gap had ballooned to 33 percent. That being said, you would be hard-pressed to find many professional matchmakers—not to mention many single, 40-something women—who would dispute the idea that the 40-year-old's marriage prospects are materially worse than the 27-year-old's.

The popular explanation is that older men forgo age-appropriate women in order to date younger women, whereas 40-year-old women either have less interest in dating younger men or less ability to entice them. The end result is a smaller pool of potential matches—and thus reduced marriage odds—for the 40-year-old woman. There is certainly some data to support the

conventional explanation: According to Census numbers, 11 percent of husbands are six to nine years older
than their wives, whereas only 3 percent of wives are six
to nine years older than their husbands. There are many
possible explanations for this. Younger women tend to
perceive older men as better providers, and older men
often perceive younger women as more attractive. (The
latter may be a misperception. According to OkTrends,
a single 35-year-old woman is generally percieved as no
less attractive than a single 25-year-old. The operative
word here, though, is "single," as many married women
"have stopped optimizing their attractiveness," OkTrends
claimed, whereas the single 35-year-olds are still "optimizing.") Finally, women's biological clocks play a role as
well: A man who wants five kids is probably not going to
marry a 40-year-old woman.

Thing is, if older women's dating struggles were
completely a function of older men dating younger
women, then there should be a second cohort of struggling
daters. There should be a large cadre of early-to-mid-
twenties, college-educated men who are starved for
female companionship because the women their age are
all being poached by older men. In other words, 25-year-
old guys should be just as frustrated as 40-year-old
women. "Yeah, I've wondered about that one myself," said
Sandra Ferry,* a 50-year-old venture capital executive
who began our interview grumbling about her ex-
husband remarrying someone twenty years his junior.
"The young guys who work for me don't seem to be

having any trouble." Indeed, according to OkTrends, 26 is actually the age of peak desirability for men—as measured by the percentage of the single women interested in dating them.

Another familiar take on the dating woes of 40-year-old women is that these woes are largely a myth—a falsehood popularized by the mainstream media in order to scare women and sell dating books and magazines. The starting point for this line of thinking is usually an infamous *Newsweek* cover story published in 1986. The article, titled "The Marriage Crunch," contained the dubious claim that a single, college-educated woman over 40 was "more likely to be killed by a terrorist" than to find a husband.

The *Newsweek* article was a serious look at the marriage squeeze afflicting Baby Boomer women—the same statistical phenomenon Guttentag had examined. Unfortunately, the story's credibility was torpedoed by an editing blunder: A sentence in an internal memo that was intended as a joke—the terrorist quip—was accidentally inserted into the final copy by a careless editor. *Newsweek*'s official correction came twenty years after the fact and prompted critics to cast doubt on the story's entire premise. A writer for *The Wall Street Journal*, Jeffrey Zaslow, reinterviewed ten of the fourteen single women featured in the *Newsweek* story and found eight had gotten married and two remained single by choice. He also cited demographic data showing that more women from the Baby Boomer generation had eventually married than the *Newsweek* article originally predicted. "If they want to get married," Zaslow told ABC News, "women can get married."

Had Zaslow dug a little deeper into the data he would have discovered that the marriage squeeze was no myth. Yes, single baby boomer women wound up getting married at a higher-than-expected rate. But that was only because men responded to the imbalanced marriage market much the same way the male cichlids responded in the sex-ratio experiment: The men re-mated. An increasing number of Baby Boomer men divorced their first wives in order to wed never-married women and start second families.

The Census data tells the full story: Among those age 60 to 74—the same Baby Boomer cohort examined by *Newsweek* and by Zaslow—there are now 4 million divorced women who have not remarried versus only 2.8 million divorced-and-not-remarried men. Based on those numbers, it is apparent that a rising divorce rate for women—from 15 percent in 1970 to 21 percent in 1985—simply shifted the marriage squeeze from single women who were never married to single women who were divorced.

So if the worsening marriage prospects of 40-year-old women are not a myth and are not a function (at least primarily) of 40-year-old men dating 30-year-old women, what, then, is the primary cause? The answer lies in simple mathematics. The best way to visualize this is as a dating-game version of musical chairs. If you played musical chairs as a child, you probably barely even noticed that there was a chair missing in the first round—when, say, there were 25 players and 24 chairs. Everyone but the paste-eaters and the butterfly-chasers got a chair in the first round. By the end of the game, however, the chances of not getting a chair had risen dramatically—from 4 percent when there were 24 chairs left to 50 percent when there was just one. Each time a chair was removed, the chances of losing the game increased.

Just as with musical chairs, it is a mathematical certainty that the marriage prospects will worsen for college-grad women the longer they stay in the dating game. Today's 40-year-old, college-educated woman started out in a dating pool with 117 women for every 100 men, or 17 percent more women than men—not good numbers but certainly better than the 134 women for every 100 men confronting recent grads. However, once two-thirds of the men in the 40-year-old's original dating pool had gotten married, the remaining single women were confronted by a far more daunting marriage market, one with 50 women for every 33 men. (I've rounded up.) That's 52 percent more women than men.

As challenging as the numbers may be for today's 40-year-old women, the dating math will be even harder on college-educated, millennial women as *they* hit their thirties (at least assuming they intend on marrying college-educated men). Young millennials are starting out in a dating pool with 134 women for every 100 men. By the time two-thirds of the men are married, the dating pool for the remaining singles will become 67 women for every 33 men—or two women for every one man. And after 25 more of those men marry, the remaining dating pool becomes 5 women for every one man. In such an environment, those millennial men who remain single into their thirties will have even less incentive to settle down.

The bottom line is that in a dating market in which men are in low supply, a woman who delays marriage until she's 40 is indeed taking a greater risk of ending up alone. For the college-educated woman who puts an extremely high priority on getting married to a college-educated man, she may be better off strategically—though not necessarily romantically—getting married young to Mr. Perfectly Acceptable rather than holding out till 40 for Mr. Right.

Another dating-market quirk that confused me even more than the general oversupply of 30-something and 40-something women is who these women tend to be. In my experience, a disproportionate number of the women who claim to have the most difficulty dating after 30 are those who have the most going for them. They are smart, fun, kind, and attractive. A lot of them are probably more physically fit at 40 than they were at 24. It's no wonder friends and family assume these women are either too picky or are just plain terrible at dating.

In contrast to the single women, the over-30 men I know who are single—and to be honest, I know few—tend to be men I'd be reluctant to fix up with my female friends. Some are unemployed or unattractive or womanizers or asexual (and perhaps closeted) or some combination of the above.

I am not the first to observe this incongruity in the over-30 dating market. Writing in *Slate* in 2008, Bloomberg News editor Mark Gimein used auction theory to explain why, as singles hit their thirties, the number of attractive women seemed to increase even as the pool of appealing men seemed to decline. "In this auction," Gimein wrote, "some women will be more confident of their prospects, others less so." In the jargon of auction theory, the first group are "strong bidders" and the latter "weak bidders." Conventional wisdom holds that the strong bidders would be far more likely to win this kind of competition, given that women with good looks, social skills, or other perceived strengths are generally considered to be more of a catch. But that's not how real auctions play out, according to Gimein. "In fact," he wrote, "game theory predicts, and empirical studies of auctions bear out, that auctions will often be won by 'weak' bidders, who know that they can be outbid and so bid more aggressively."

In the marriage market, the strong bidder frequently holds out for the ideal mate—not unlike the billionaire art collector at Sotheby's who passes on the Bérauds and Boudins in order to vie for the lone van Gogh. "With a lot at stake in getting it right in one shot," wrote Gimein, "it's the women who are confident that they are holding a strong hand who are likely to hold out and wait for the perfect prospect."

This explains why a disproportionate number of the women who are still single in their thirties are so attractive and marriageable, while a disproportionate number of the remaining men seem to be unattractive, socially awkward, emotionally damaged, or unemployed. Gimein concluded that the good men really are taken. They married *young*—"to women whose most salient characteristic was not their beauty or passion or intellect, but their decisiveness."

I mentioned Gimein's theory—that in a man-deficit world, it is the assertive women who get the guys—to Jeffrey Sirkman, the rabbi at Larchmont Temple, a Reform Jewish synagogue in suburban New York. Having married and counseled hundreds of college-educated couples over his twenty-five-year career, Sirkman is a keen observer of the marriage market, and he's long wondered why so many great women struggle to find husbands. Sirkman told me that of the nine soon-to-be-married young couples he was then counseling, seven shared a similar story. "The men all had several options," Sirkman said, "and the women they ended up marrying were the ones who pursued them most aggressively." Indeed, the long-held stereotype that men enjoy the chase—a theory that drives dating guides like *The Rules* and countless other dating strategies—may well be a myth. Men want to be wanted, and in a lopsided dating market, women who are pursuers are more likely to succeed than those who sit back and wait for Mr. Right to woo them.

A few years ago, I had lunch with my friend Sarah Donovan—as I mentioned, one of those everything-going-for-her women whose single status is so baffling. About to turn 38 at the time, Sarah had been dating the same guy, Matt, for about two years. Sarah and I are more work friends than personal friends, but the last time she had mentioned Matt, it certainly sounded like all was well and they were on their way to getting married. After our drinks arrived, I asked about Matt. "We broke up," she sighed. One of those a-bit-too-perfect 45-year-olds who'd just never quite found the right girl, Matt had revealed to Sarah some vague "fear" about the future and announced that he just was not ready to settle down.

My initial reaction to this story was exasperation. It seemed cruel for a guy to date a woman in her late thirties for two years without marrying her. Yet as I would learn from interviews with single women and professional matchmakers, these guys are a dime a dozen in cities like New York. "I call them 'time thieves,'" said Manhattan matchmaker Avgitidis.

The more Sarah and I talked, the more I began to wonder why she had not given Matt a marriage ultimatum earlier in the relationship. Sarah wanted kids, and she knew her biological clock was ticking. So why let things drag on for two years? The irony was that Sarah actually had two married friends who got engaged only after issuing ultimatums to their own boyfriends. These were both couples where the men seemed the most devoted and the most over the moon and where the women were anything but the forceful, aggressive types. Yet each woman had to put her foot down and essentially demand a ring in order to get one.

Sarah wanted her guy to come around on his own, and many dating experts seem to think this is the best approach. "Giving your boyfriend an ultimatum isn't going to change his response," wrote TheFrisky.com advice columnist Wendy Atterberry when counseling one would-be ultimatum maker. "The only thing an ultimatum will do is eliminate one of your options."

The problem with such advice is it assumes that the decision-making process for romance has little in common with the process by which human beings make every other type of important decision. A common refrain in business and politics is that it is unwise to make a decision any sooner than you have to. College-educated men who equivocate about getting married are, on some level, acting rationally: Why make a lifetime commitment to one woman when you can keep her as an option while continuing to survey the market—a market that, for college-educated men, has an ever-increasing number of options?

Ultimatums work because they create artificial scarcity in an otherwise abundant marketplace. They make us want more what we fear we may lose. "When increasing scarcity [interferes] with our prior access to some item, we will react against the interference by wanting and trying to possess the item more than before," wrote Robert Cialdini, an Arizona State University marketing and psychology professor, in *Influence*, a classic text on the art of persuasion.

In *Bargaining for Advantage*, another book on the topic, Richard Shell, a professor at UPenn's Wharton

School, tells a story involving Wayne Huizenga, the Florida business mogul who founded Waste Management, Blockbuster, and AutoNation. Huizenga and his partner were in a law-firm conference room, about to close on the purchase of a family-owned business for $4 million, when a dispute arose over the fate of $100,000 in the business's bank account. Huizenga wanted the money included in the deal, but the seller was refusing to part with it.

Huizenga's response? "Okay boys, let's go home," he said as he packed up his briefcase and led his team out of the room.

"Wayne, are you crazy?" Huizenga's business partner pleaded as they walked away. "Over one hundred thousand dollars?"

"They're never going to let us get to the elevator," Huizenga whispered—just before the lawyer for the other side darted out of the conference room and announced that his client would relent.

Huizenga's strategy worked because he was willing to walk away. This may sound high-risk (not to mention manipulative) when applied to marriage. But there is strong evidence that women who are prepared to break things off are, in fact, more likely to get a ring. John Molloy, a management consultant and author of *Why Men Marry Some Women and Not Others*, assigned a team of researchers to interview 3,000 U.S. couples right after they got their marriage licenses. Of the women interviewed, 60 percent said they were prepared to walk away if their men suddenly announced that they weren't ready to get married.

☗☗☗☗

Karen Peterson*—a friend from my hometown and probably the most attractive person I know—complained to me a few years back that she had not been asked out on a date in months. Had someone been eavesdropping on our conversation, the comment surely would have sounded preposterous. Peterson looks like a 40-something Scarlett Johansson. I did not doubt the genuineness of Peterson's complaint, however, simply because I had heard too many other stories of beautiful women being ignored by men they were interested in.

Why does this happen? Jose-Manuel Rey, a mathematics professor at Universidad Complutense de Madrid, used statistics, probability theory, and a fictitious case study involving a guy named Guy in order to explain the phenomenon. In Rey's scenario, Guy is sitting at a coffee shop reading the newspaper when he spots Carol, a beautiful woman to whom he's attracted, sitting at a nearby table. For Guy, there are three possible outcomes:

1. He talks to Carol, she responds positively, and he gets her phone number and a proper date the following Friday.
2. He does nothing and continues enjoying his coffee.
3. He talks to Carol, she's not interested, and he winds up feeling miserable about being rejected.

The problem for Carol—assuming she too is interested—is that Guy cannot consider these three possible outcomes in a vacuum. He can only consider them in the context of all the other men at the coffee shop who also may want to approach Carol—which makes this, in Rey's words, "an interactive decision problem." Rey runs through some fancy math to reach his conclusions—read it all at http://plus.maths.org/content/carol-syndrome—but the bottom line is that the more admirers Guy perceives Carol to have, the less likely it is that Guy or any other man will approach her.

Guy and the rest of the men in the coffee shop all assume that the third outcome—being rejected—is the likeliest one simply because there's only one Carol and so many of them. The odds are not in any one man's favor. "Carol's perception that she scares men away is not a delusion after all," wrote Rey. "It is not a matter of bad luck but a collateral effect of interactive rationality. A paradoxical consequence is that Carol's attractiveness acts as a repellent. This surprising phenomenon—which we call the *Carol syndrome*—is a by-product of psychological social interaction."

Margaret Kent, the author of the 1987 bestseller *How to Marry the Man of Your Choice*—a guide to what many might call psychologically manipulative tactics designed to lure men into marriage—saw attractive women befuddled by this all the time. They are the ones who came to her most often for help, she wrote, while those she called "Denny's Darlings" or "the toothless wonders at the donut shop" didn't seem to need any help at all. Perhaps not coincidentally, the cities most affected by the man deficit—New York, Miami, etc.—tend to have a lot of Carols and other "strong bidders." In those cities, the payoff can be enormous for men willing to make the first move with their Carols.

After many months of poring through Census data, one of my more puzzling findings involved the marriage prospects of Asian American women. In the U.S., 67 percent of Asian American women age 30 to 34 have a college degree, versus 38 percent for all women. Given that they are disproportionately college educated, I had assumed that Asian American women would be far *more* affected by the man deficit than women from other racial or ethnic groups.

My assumption proved dead wrong. Asian American women are basically immune to the man deficit. They have no trouble finding husbands. An astounding 88 percent of Asian American women in the 30-to-34 age bracket are married or have been married compared to 77 percent for white women, 73 percent for Hispanic women, and 46 percent for black women.

It wasn't always this way. Back in 1986, Asian American women in their early thirties had a much lower marriage rate than white women did—74 percent versus 89 percent. (The Census Bureau definition of "Asian" refers to people having origins in the Far East, Southeast Asia, or the Indian subcontinent, including Cambodia, China, India, Japan, Korea, Malaysia, Pakistan, the Philippine Islands, Thailand, and Vietnam.)

What changed since 1986? The simplest answer is that Asian American women have become more desirable to non–Asian American men. My 42-year-old-friend Erica Jenkins* is half Chinese, and her experience growing up was that the boys in her mostly white high school had little interest in dating Asian American girls. "It was not good to be an Asian girl," said Jenkins. At some point in the 1990s, however, she noticed a positive change in men's perception of Asian American women. For Jenkins, the cultural touchstone for this shift was a 1994 episode of *Seinfeld* titled "The Chinese Woman." In the episode, Jerry is thrilled to be going on a blind date with a woman named Donna Chang.

"I love Chinese women," Jerry tells Elaine.

Elaine: "Isn't that a little racist?"

"If I like their race," replies Jerry, "how can that be racist?"

It can, of course. The punch line—and Jerry's eventual comeuppance—occurs at the end of the episode, when Jerry discovers that Donna Chang is not Chinese at all. She is a white woman from Long Island whose family had shortened their name to Chang from Changstein.

For my purposes, it doesn't really matter why men perceive Asian American women as especially desirable. Whether the root cause is racial stereotype or biology, what's important is that this racial preference is real. Men of all races do indeed perceive Asian women as most attractive, according to psychological experiments conducted by Michael Lewis, a professor of cognitive science at Cardiff University in the U.K. OkCupid's OkTrends data blog reached the same conclusion using online dating data.

OkTrends analyzed the response rates that people receive on OkCupid when they send introductory messages to men and women of varying racial backgrounds. According to OkTrends, men were, on average, more likely to respond to messages from Asian American women than from women of any other ethnic group other than Middle Eastern women (who, according to OkTrends, were less likely to date outside their ethnicity and were presumably sending a disproportionate number of messages to Middle Eastern men).

The average male response rate to messages from Asian American females was 44 percent, versus a 42 percent average for all women on OkCupid. Asian American men responded to them at a 48 percent clip. White men responded to messages from Asian American women at the same rate (41 percent) that they responded to messages from white women. African American and Hispanic men were actually more likely to respond to messages from Asian American women (55 percent and 49 percent response rates, respectively) than from women of their own race (37 percent and 48 percent). The allure of Asian American women even held true among lesbians: Messages sent by Asian American lesbians had a 53 percent response rate from other lesbians on OkCupid versus an average response rate of 50 percent for all lesbian message senders.

Desirability isn't Asian American women's only dating-market advantage. They also benefit from the fact that Asian American men are as disfavored as Asian American women are favored. Asian American men on OkCupid get only a 22 percent message response rate from women, the lowest response rate on the website. The average response rate for messages sent by all men on OkCupid is 27 percent, with white men faring best, at 29 percent.

What this shows is that Asian American women have decisive advantages in both the intra-racial and interracial dating markets. Asian American women are favored by men of all races, whereas Asian American men have more limited dating options outside of their race.

"Oh, I would never approach a group of Asian girls in a bar. I know this is going to sound bad, but they're mean," said Steve Sharma,* a single, 39-year-old college grad of Indian descent currently living in New York. "They know they have the upper hand.

"Which means they're much, much choosier."

Chapter 8
Solving the Man Deficit

....

There are excellent reasons why this is *not* a dating-advice book. Nobody considers me an authority on matters of the heart, and I am certainly no expert on courtship or on the darker arts of seduction. More to the point, I recognize that marriage and romance need not be top priorities for everyone, which is why one-size-fits-all advice on how single men and women should navigate today's lopsided dating markets seems foolish. A woman who dreams of ruling Wall Street or a man who wants to be the next Mark Zuckerberg is not going to pass on living in New York City or Silicon Valley just because local gender ratios may be skewed against them.

That said, I do believe that good decisions are informed ones. And the sad reality is that many singles today have no clue that they are participating in a lopsided dating market, which means some of them wind up making important life decisions based on faulty assumptions. One 43-year-old woman I interviewed—someone who always wanted children—admitted to me that she might have said yes to a man who had proposed fifteen years earlier had she known how stacked the marriage market was against her. With that in mind, here are five gender-ratio-related *suggestions*, all aimed at helping men and women make better-informed life decisions.

I. Make gender ratios a consideration when choosing college.

For heterosexual young men who are shy and awkward, four years at a school like Sarah Lawrence or Skidmore College (64 percent female) might do wonders for their self-confidence.

For heterosexual women, the stakes are higher. Given the social dynamics at colleges that are disproportionately female, young women evaluating colleges may want to think carefully about whether attending a school with a 60:40 gender ratio—or even one that's 58:42—would be a good fit for them. Academically, no doubt there are many great reasons to attend schools such as University of Georgia or New York University; there may even be social benefits for young women who want to experiment sexually while still in college. However, if a young woman is concerned or unenthusiastic about the hookup culture, attending such a school may be consigning herself to four very unhappy years.

A college-bound high school girl in Georgia, for example, might think twice about attending University of Georgia and consider making Georgia Institute of Technology her top choice instead. The in-state tuitions at the two schools are similar: $5,623 at UGA vs. $5,873 at Georgia Tech, according to *The Washington Post*'s StudentAdvisor.com website, which lets users compare key metrics for most colleges and universities. Georgia Tech—which offers liberal arts degrees as well as degrees in math and sciences—actually has a slightly higher acceptance rate (58 percent versus 53 percent) as well as higher average SAT scores (1,230 vs. 1,130). More to the point, Georgia Tech is 66 percent male, UGA is 62 percent female, and their respective gender ratios have a major influence on campus life. According to niche.com, a student-authored college review site, Georgia Tech is "fairly monogamous" and "people like to be in a relationship," whereas at UGA, "hookups occur rampantly" and "the walk of shame is pretty common for many students."

The calculus is similar for women applying to private colleges. Yes, NYU is terrific academically, but the hookup culture there and at many other 60:40 schools is so over the top that it prompted NYU's own associate director of counseling to raise concerns. Young women seeking a more traditional college social life might consider other selective colleges that offer better gender balance. Two such examples: Tufts University in suburban Boston and University of Rochester in Rochester, New York, both of which have 50:50 gender ratios. Thanks to strong math and science departments, those two schools attract more men. The end result: more dates and fewer hookups. "Halfway through sophomore year, people begin to pair off and generally stay paired off through junior and senior year," niche.com wrote of Tufts. "A lot of students complain that by their third year, all the guys or girls worth being with at Tufts are taken."

Here's one more thing to consider. A significant number of college-educated Americans do meet their husbands and wives in college. A 2012 study by sociologists Michael Rosenfeld of Stanford University and Ruben Thomas of City College of New York found that about 10 percent of American couples met in college or grad school. Given that 39 percent of young adults have college degrees, one can extrapolate from Rosenfeld's study and estimate that about a quarter of college-educated American couples met in college or grad school. A 2013 Facebook study came up with a similar figure—28 percent of Facebook users met their husbands or wives in college.

You don't need a degree in applied math from Georgia Tech to understand that a woman attending a college with fewer men faces lower odds of meeting her future husband in school. But one unexpected finding from the Facebook study was that the men most likely to have met their wives in college were *not* those who attended the colleges with the most women. They attended schools that were between 51 percent and 54 percent *male*—which actually makes sense. Had those men attended a college that was 60 percent female, settling down might have been the furthest thing from their minds. (For more on the connection between college dating and sex ratios, see the table on pages 188–193.)

2. Be aware that holding out is a risky marriage strategy for college-educated women.

The actual marriage odds for millennial women won't be as bad as my musical chairs scenario in Chapter 7 implies. Just like male cichlids, men respond to lopsided gender ratios by opting to re-mate. Among college grads age 30 to 39, there are 522,898 divorced-but-not-remarried women in the U.S., versus only 302,716 divorced-but-not-remarried men. As my married neighbor sometimes advises her own never-married friends: "Just wait for the second round."

While divorce could end up easing the marriage squeeze for millennials (sadly), it remains true that the marriage prospects of college-educated women decline with age. Many women—including *Otherhood* author Melanie Notkin—may prefer not to get married at all than settle for a husband lacking in the qualities important to them. I appreciate that, and what I am about to say should not be construed as a suggestion that they must settle or an implication that younger women need to choose between career and family. Everybody's life priorities are different, which means the diminished marriage odds are less important to some women than to others.

The statistical reality for millennial women, however, is that finding a college-educated husband will be much easier at age 25 or 26 than it will at age 35 or 36. Also, at the risk of stating the obvious, just because a woman marries young does not mean she must have children young too. My wife, Laura, and I married when we were both 24, and it wasn't until Laura was 31 years old—and three years into her dream job as a federal prosecutor—that we had our twins.

And while this too may be stating the obvious, dating can be as much of a time-and-attention juggle for the single career woman as family can be for the working mom. At a question-and-answer session with Facebook chief operating officer Sheryl Sandberg promoting her much-discussed book *Lean In*, one woman raised her hand and commented that for all the discussion about how hard it is for women to balance work and motherhood, it is equally hard for women rising in the workplace to juggle being single: "How can I 'lean in,'" the woman asked, "when at five p.m. I need to leave the office to go to a bar?"

3. Your workplace is part of your dating ecology, so choose your career judiciously.

The obvious caveats apply here. A man who dreams of being a famous architect should not attend nursing school simply because 90 percent of nurses are female and 75 percent of architects are male. A female elementary school teacher who is happy at her job but unlucky at love should not retrain to be an aircraft mechanic just because 98 percent of aircraft mechanics are men and 80 percent of schoolteachers are women.

Nevertheless, when young men and women first start thinking about careers, they may want to factor gender ratios into their decisions—particularly if dating is not one of their strong suits. According to the Rosenfeld study, 10 percent of couples meet at work. While I would not want to discourage young women from becoming schoolteachers or young men from becoming policemen (87 percent male), they should know going in that their career choices could dim their dating prospects. Some other professions that are overwhelmingly male include mechanical engineer (93 percent men), computer network administrator (83 percent), and financial advisor (74 percent). Science-related professions skew male generally, but the medical sciences are an exception: Medical and biological scientists are only 47 percent male. Other professions that skew female include real estate broker (58 percent female), convention and event planner (75 percent), and tax preparer (62 percent).

For a more complete look at gender ratios within various professions, go to the U.S. Bureau of Labor Statistics website, bls.gov.

4. Go West, Young Woman.

I asked Susan Weber-Stoger, a researcher and Census-data expert at Queens College, to rank some eighty U.S. counties with populations of 60,000 or more by their ratios of college-educated men to college-educated women age 22 to 29. Turns out that the land of milk and honey is also the land of men and men with money. Three of the five counties with the highest ratios of men to women were in California, as were eight of the top twenty-five. (See the table on pages 198–205.)

Santa Clara County and San Francisco County

ranked one and two, respectively. No surprise there. They were also the only counties that actually had more men than women (though a disproportionate number of San Francisco's college-grad men are likely gay, based on Williams Institute data). The third California county to make the top five, fifth-ranked San Diego County, had a mere 10 percent more female college grads than male ones (and the numbers were actually even among singles). The other California counties in the women-friendly top 25 included Alameda County (11), Marin County (15), Sacramento County (16), Sonoma County (21), and San Mateo County (22).

Interestingly, most of the man-heavy California counties also boasted disproportionately high male incomes. Nationwide, 2013 median incomes for men with college degrees and men with graduate degrees were $60,909 and $81,789, respectively. In Alameda County, it was $70,803 and $100,429. In San Mateo County, it was $72,455 and $120,586. Santa Clara County: $94,377 and $122,304.

The two non-California counties rounding out the man-heavy top five were Richmond County, New York, and Franklin County, Ohio. It is a little ironic that Richmond County—better known as Staten Island— would be the third-best large dating market in the country for college-educated women in their twenties, since it happens to be right across the harbor from another island perceived as one of the worst: Manhattan. Staten Island has 3 percent more young, educated men than women overall and 9 percent more single ones. Despite their physical proximity, however, the cultural divide between Manhattan and Staten Island is gaping. Staten Island's population is overwhelmingly white, working class, and not particularly cosmopolitan, which is why I do not expect Manhattan career women to start pouring onto the Staten Island Ferry in search of dates (though perhaps they should).

What about the best dating markets for older, college-educated singles? The two best counties for 30-something women—i.e., the places with the highest ratios of single college-educated men to single college-educated women among those age 30 to 39—are Muscogee County, Georgia (which is where Columbus and Fort Benning are located), and Santa Clara County. The two best for men are Durham County, North Carolina, and Sonoma County, California. Sonoma's status is interesting because it means Sonoma boasts a high (or at least not-so-low) ratio of men to women for 20-somethings to go along with a very low ratio of men to women for 30-somethings. The obvious takeaway here is that Sonoma's 27-year-old men should be asking out the 33-year-old women on dates—and vice versa.

For college-grad singles age 40 to 49, the best two counties for women are Polk County, Iowa (county seat: Des Moines), and Travis County, Texas (Austin, the county seat, is the high-tech hub of the southwest). The two best for men are Fort Bend County, Texas (a suburb of Houston), and Utah County, Utah (home to Provo and BYU).

For college-educated singles age 50 to 59, Anchorage

County, Alaska, has the highest ratio of men to women, followed by San Francisco County. The two best counties for single men are both in Georgia: Bibb County—county seat: Macon—ranks first, followed by Gwinnett County, which is a suburb of Atlanta.

5. College-educated women should consider expanding their dating pool to include lesser-educated men.

Some millennial women may have no choice. For them, the marriage math will never add up, not with 134 recent female college grads for every 100 male ones. There is simply no way that all the college-educated women who wish to marry college-educated men can do so— not unless there is an unprecedented spike in the divorce rate. My prediction is that we will be hearing much more in coming years about the rise of what I call the mixed-collar marriage—professional women married to working-class men.

Such pairings are already commonplace in the African American community, where the college gender gap is extreme. According to the NCES, 112,898 African American women graduated from four-year colleges in 2011, versus 59,119 African American men. As a result, educated African American women who wish to marry within their own race have little choice but to consider dating less educated African American men.

Black pop culture reflects this demographic reality. Beyoncé (who grew up in a wealthy Houston suburb) makes dating down sound downright sexy in songs such as "Suga Mama" and "Upgrade U." And mixed-collar relationships are a staple of Tyler Perry movies: In *The Family That Preys*, Harvard-educated Andrea is married to hunky construction worker Chris, and in *Daddy's Little Girls*, romance blooms between attorney Julia and muscle-bound mechanic Monty. Cleveland matchmaker Tammie Collins, who is African American, told me that mixed-collar pairings were "definitely" more common among her black clients than among white ones. A 2010 Pew Research report reflected the same reality: 33 percent of African American women were married to men with less education, compared to 28 percent of all American women.

To be sure, some college-educated women might balk at the idea of marrying a working-class man. However, others could view a mixed-collar marriage as a solution to a modern dilemma—the career woman who could really use a partner with more time to help with homework or attend Little League games. Plus, there's evidence that American men and women of all hues are increasingly comfortable with reversed gender roles. According to the same Pew Research study, 30 percent of married women were primary breadwinners in 2007, versus just 4 percent in 1960.

The bottom line is that in a city like New York, single women may have more success meeting good men at a fireman's pub in Staten Island than at a wine bar on the Upper East Side. Indeed, if there were one investable idea to come out of this book, it would involve setting up a dating agency or online dating site that breaks through social barriers and matches college-educated women with appealing, non-college-educated men. An improved economy—one that lifted the earnings and job security of working-class men—would go a long way toward making those matches more viable.

All of these suggestions are geared toward beating today's dating odds rather than actually changing them. There is only one way to fix the man deficit, and that involves more men attending college. Public colleges and universities cannot achieve this on their own, since affirmative action for men would violate Title IX. Private colleges do have leeway under Title IX to accept more men, but few want to be caught using it. One college that did acknowledge favoring boys is Kenyon College. In a 2006 *New York Times* op-ed piece titled "To All the Girls I've Rejected," Kenyon College dean of admissions Jennifer Delahunty Britz said she had to give preference to male candidates in order to keep Kenyon's gender ratio below 60:40. "The elephant that looms large in the middle of the room is gender balance," wrote Britz. "The reality is that because young men are rarer, they're more valued applicants."

Britz's column caused a small uproar—which is probably why other private colleges have kept silent on the subject ever since. "If I was a man at Kenyon, I'd be thinking about transferring," penned a writer from *The Nation*. "I wouldn't want people to think I needed a boost just because I was male. And I wouldn't want to wonder if maybe I DID need a boost. I might even feel guilty that I had deprived a better candidate—you know, one of those brilliant poetry-writing future-vaccine-discovering change-the-world-for-the-better girls Dean Britz describes rejecting. I might have to go to a slightly less selective college, but that would be okay: I would have my self-esteem!"

Even if more private colleges were to embrace affirmative action for men, it would make only a modest dent in the man deficit, since only 40 percent of U.S. college students attend private colleges. Short of changing Title IX or skirting the law, there is no short-term fix to the college gender gap. The only true solutions are long-term ones—improving the academic performance of high school boys and combating the maturity issues that knock some teenage boys off the college track.

There has been plenty written on the ADHD scourge as well as on the various ways that contemporary school curricula may disadvantage boys. The best-known book on this subject is *The War Against Boys* by Christina Hoff Sommers, a former philosophy professor who is now a resident scholar at the American Enterprise Institute. Personally, I have little interest in diving into the culture war Sommers is waging on this issue. Sommers does a great job illuminating all the various ways boys fall short of girls academically, but her solutions feel underwhelming. As the parent of one organizationally challenged teenage boy, I'm dubious that more recess or more focus on organizational skills would make a significant impact. My son's middle school teachers and guidance counselors all worked diligently with him on organizational skills. But it wasn't until my son was a little older and more mature that he got better at remembering not only to do his homework . . . but to actually hand it in too. Boy-friendly reading assignments (*The Natural* instead of *The Pearl*, perhaps?) and more time for recess might help on the margins, but pedagogical reforms cannot change the biological reality that girls are more mature socially and intellectually than boys of the same age.

So what, then, is the solution? Scholarly research has shown that boys typically lag one year behind girls in social skills and in brain development. Consequently, boys who are held back a year—boys who start first grade at age 7 instead of age 6—tend to fare better academically. In one study, Sandra Crosser, an education professor at Ohio Northern University, found evidence of significant test-score improvement for fifth- and sixth-grade boys who had started school a year late but no such improvement for late-starting girls. Kelly Bedard and Elizabeth Dhuey, economics professors at University of California, Santa Barbara and the University of Toronto, found that high school students considered old for their grade—i.e., students who complete junior year of high school at age 18—not only earned better grades than younger peers but were also 12 percent more likely to attend college. Patrick McEwan and Joseph Shapiro, economics professors at Wellesley and MIT, studied educational data from Chile and found that the test-score improvement was one-third larger for boys considered old for their grade than for older girls.

Leonard Sax, a leading expert on gender differences in child development and author of the influential *Boys Adrift*, has gone so far as to suggest that boys be held back two years, not just one—particularly if reading is going to be taught in kindergarten. "Waiting until seven years of age to begin the formal, 'rigorous,' reading and writing curriculum of today's kindergarten might reduce or ameliorate a significant fraction of the problems we see with boys and school," wrote Sax, a family physician and psychologist. "For many boys, there's a huge difference in readiness to learn between age five and age seven—just as there's a huge difference in readiness for a girl between three and five."

A two-year delay for boys sounds like a bit much, but there is anecdotal evidence from other Western countries that a one-year delay could help narrow the college gender gap. Consider Finland and Switzerland. In those two countries, most children do not begin first grade until age 7, and, according to data from the World Bank, Finland and Switzerland both boast smaller gender imbalances in higher education than do Australia, the U.K., the U.S., and other Western countries where kids generally start first grade at age 6. In Switzerland, the gender ratio in higher education is actually 50:50. Bottom line: Give boys more time to mature, and they do seem to do a better job keeping pace with girls.

Delaying when boys start kindergarten or first grade may shrink the man deficit, but it would not be a silver bullet. It would not alter the fact that boys have greater access to higher-paying jobs right out of high school. Also, it could create a thorny new set of problems for parents and for school administrators, as more 19-year-old young men would be interacting socially in high school with girls who are 15 or 16. Moreover, delaying when boys start first grade is not something states or school districts in the U.S. could implement from the top down, since different rules for boys than girls would violate Title IX. Change would have to come from the bottom up, via a grassroots movement among parents of boys. Such a movement is theoretically possible, though, since most school districts do give parents the leeway to delay when their children start school.

Holding back boys is one long-term solution to the man deficit. Another would be allowing the free market to run its course. As I said at the outset, few men and women appreciate the sizable impact that gender ratios have on their sex lives, their marriage prospects, and their happiness. Perhaps this book will help change that. Perhaps more young men will aspire to college. Perhaps more professional women will be open to dating electricians and police officers—men who may not earn as much as lawyers or stockbrokers but may be more interested in settling down.

Something has to give. Any market inefficiency that allows one group to take advantage of another is not sustainable so long as that inefficiency derives from discoverable information. Just ask Billy Beane, the Oakland A's general manager who was the star of *Moneyball*. The A's posted a .620 winning percentage for the three seasons before *Moneyball* was published in 2003, versus .560 for the three teams Beane assembled after author Michael Lewis revealed the A's trade secrets.

The dating market will prove no different. Boys who like sex will try harder to get into college. Boys who really like sex will apply to Sarah Lawrence. And educated women who wish to improve their marriage prospects will date down or will quit Manhattan for Silicon Valley or some other locale where the demographics are more favorable. Over time, the dating market will return to equilibrium.

How much time? It took only a few years for *Moneyball* to change baseball. But this change, I suspect, will probably take a little longer.

APPENDIX

HOW COLLEGE GENDER RATIOS AFFECT COLLEGE DATING

This table ranks 35 private and public colleges and universities by their gender ratios, while also including students' own descriptions of campus dating life. (The gender-ratio data comes from studentadvisor.com; the descriptions of dating life are pulled from niche.com, a student-authored college review website.) Yes, casual sex in college is nothing new. And yes, the student comments I selected are some of the more colorful ones. But as this table demonstrates, monogamy is more commonplace on campuses with either gender balance or more men than women, whereas the hookup culture is more prevalent at colleges that are disproportionately female.

COLLEGE	% WOMEN	% MEN
Rensselaer Polytechnic Institute Troy, NY	28%	72%
"More people are involved in relationships . . . [Girls] seem to become stuck up because they're in such a minority that they can afford to be very choosy."		
Georgia Institute of Technology Atlanta, GA	34%	66%
"Tech is a fairly monogamous campus . . . [F]or the most part, people like to be in relationships."		
California Institute of Technology Pasadena, CA	41%	59%
"Students here tend not to date but have relationships . . . [B]reakups are rare, and many couples get married after CalTech."		

Drexel University   45%   55%
Philadelphia, PA

"Hookups are inevitable at any university, but it seems as though many Drexel students are involved in relatively low-key relationships."

University of Colorado   47%   53%
Boulder, CO

"Guys often complain that these picturesque women show little remorse for the men who fail to satisfy their expensive taste."

University of Chicago   48%   52%
Chicago, IL

"Some people date seriously, and if you kiss someone on the bridge over Botany Pond, you'll marry them."

Stanford University   48%   52%
Palo Alto, CA

"There is a lot of 'going steady' . . . but there is also a hookup culture."

Johns Hopkins University   49%   51%
Baltimore, MD

"By sophomore year, there are less hookups and more relationships."

University of Rochester   50%   50%
Rochester, NY

"At the beginning, there's a flurry of hookups, though it tends to taper off as the year progresses."

University of Michigan   50%   50%
Ann Arbor, MI

"If you're seeking a relationship, chances are you'll find the person you're looking for."

Tufts University   50%   50%
Medford, MA
"Halfway through sophomore year, people begin to pair off and generally stay paired off through junior and senior year."

Harvard University   50%   50%
Cambridge, MA
"Annoyingly cute couples walk the yard surprisingly often . . . Harvard *[alumni magazine] is always filled with news of Harvard newlyweds."*

University of Miami   52%   48%
Miami, FL
"Random hookups are common in the beginning, but after a few months or a year, relationships take over."

Brown University   53%   47%
Providence, RI
"Students chose between serial relationships, random hookups, or celibacy."

University of Oklahoma   53%   47%
Norman, OK
"Hookups are very common . . . but relationships are just as common. A lot of OU students find a significant other while at school, and many students get engaged or married before graduation."

University of Texas   54%   46%
Austin, TX
"The people who want to be in relationships, at least the guys, are in them. Most guys want hookups (not to say that girls don't want them, as well)."

University of Washington   55%   45%
Seattle, WA

"Underclassmen are more likely to stay single and have casual hookups. . . . Toward the tail-end of college, a lot more people seem to pair off."

University of California, San Diego   55%   45%
San Diego, CA

"[T]here are a large number of students in relationships. . . . For [others], a hookup at a bar or party one night is all they're looking for."

University of Virginia   56%   44%
Charlottesville, VA

"You'll find two types of people: those who randomly hook up at frat parties and bars, and those who are in extremely serious relationships . . ."

University of Delaware   57%   43%
Newark, DE

"Most people spend the first year or two making random hookups and going just a little bit crazy."

University of Florida   58%   42%
Gainesville, FL

"[I]n most circles, there isn't exactly a prejudice against more random hookups."

Providence College   58%   42%
Providence, RI

"One disheartening and noticeable trend is the demise of dating. [D]runken hookups—commitment-free of course—are in the vanguard."

University of California, Los Angeles   59%   41%
Los Angeles, CA

"Plenty of students merely hook up on weekends, while others settle down into quite serious relationships."

Elon University   59%   41%
Elon, NC

"Hookups are common, but by junior and senior year, many students settle down."

University of North Carolina   60%   40%
Chapel Hill, NC

"Unless you want a frat boy who (probably) doesn't want a relationship anyway, the supply of decent straight guys is pretty low."

New York University   61%   39%
New York, NY

"[Guys] take advantage of . . . the male-to-female ratio . . . and most have no plans of settling into a long-term relationship. . . ."

University of Georgia   62%   38%
Athens, GA

"Hookups occur rampantly at the bar scene downtown. . . . [T]he walk of shame is pretty common for many students."

Connecticut College   62%   38%
New London, CT

"Dances . . . provide more than ample opportunity for both sexes to find a potential hookup buddy. If you like to take it slow in relationships, however, Conn may not be the place for you."

Rollins College   62%   38%
Winter Park, FL

"At Rollins, commitment-free hookups are common and quite accepted."

Boston University   62%   38%
Boston, MA

"Freshman year is a sexual explosion. . . . There are girls to go around, and around again."

James Madison University   63%   37%
Harrisonburg, VA

"[The] deficiency of guys creates a scene that tends to embrace random hookups."

Skidmore College   64%   36%
Saratoga Springs, NY

"There are more casual hookups than relationships . . . there are only so many guys for all of these girls!"

Hampshire College   65%   35%
Amherst, MA

"[S]tudents find a social atmosphere that enables and even encourages experimentation. . . . As a result, casual hookups far outnumber more traditional pairings."

Howard University   69%   31%
Washington, D.C.

"There is a seemingly constant need to snag the 'few good guys.' . . . The Howard culture makes it easier for hookups."

Sarah Lawrence College   75%   25%
Bronxville, NY

"[T]he girls complain about loneliness, the guys get more than they can handle . . . and mindless, one-night stands are rampant."

DATING MARKETS BY STATE

Among under-40 college grads, gender ratios become somewhat less lopsided—i.e., more woman-friendly—as you move from the East Coast to the West Coast. Some notable exceptions: Alaska, Maine, and Montana.

STATE	college-grad women, age 22–29	college-grad men, age 22–29	% more college-grad women than men, age 22–29	
Alabama	67,607	45,390	49%	
Alaska	9,416	4,017	134%	
Arizona	87,761	63,559	38%	
Arkansas	36,208	24,251	49%	
California	639,398	531,085	20%	
Colorado	105,513	87,853	20%	
Connecticut	70,317	56,346	25%	
Washington, D.C.	41,975	31,315	34%	
Delaware	14,423	10,006	44%	
Florida	251,985	183,847	37%	
Georgia	147,600	99,815	48%	
Hawaii	26,780	13,864	93%	
Idaho	18,582	13,875	34%	
Illinois	280,372	205,588	36%	
Indiana	95,699	73,852	30%	
Iowa	60,955	44,200	38%	
Kansas	47,860	35,068	36%	
Kentucky	58,337	41,500	41%	
Louisiana	70,041	48,188	45%	
Maine	15,353	13,409	14%	
Maryland	131,014	96,584	36%	
Massachusetts	182,121	141,664	29%	
Michigan	143,153	103,392	38%	
Minnesota	112,665	84,226	34%	

	college-grad women, age 30–39	college-grad men, age 30–39	% more college-grad women than men, age 30–39
AL	93,464	68,257	37%
AK	13,836	11,046	25%
AZ	122,147	111,484	10%
AR	49,571	39,526	25%
CA	931,801	829,787	12%
CO	157,361	137,911	14%
CT	93,084	77,073	21%
DC	35,049	35,226	-1%
DE	22,353	15,947	40%
FL	363,262	296,377	23%
GA	234,307	175,939	33%
HI	35,162	26,016	35%
ID	32,544	26,439	23%
IL	356,180	285,467	25%
IN	128,984	96,901	33%
IA	68,572	56,321	22%
KS	63,947	56,681	13%
KY	84,376	62,421	35%
LA	88,134	64,069	38%
ME	26,799	18,562	44%
MD	179,579	140,123	28%
MA	208,895	178,606	17%
MI	196,306	159,483	23%
MN	155,140	115,742	34%

STATE	college-grad women, age 22–29	college-grad men, age 22–29	% more college-grad women than men, age 22–29
Mississippi	32,909	21,387	54%
Missouri	101,851	72,682	40%
Montana	16,339	10,742	52%
Nebraska	36,451	28,772	27%
Nevada	30,665	22,812	34%
New Hampshire	23,649	19,378	22%
New Jersey	185,515	143,997	29%
New Mexico	23,279	17,300	35%
New York	492,902	378,126	30%
North Carolina	153,517	108,512	41%
North Dakota	14,409	8,479	70%
Ohio	178,863	141,358	27%
Oklahoma	57,047	39,239	45%
Oregon	62,321	43,991	42%
Pennsylvania	253,883	192,071	32%
Rhode Island	19,953	16,012	25%
South Carolina	63,242	49,114	29%
South Dakota	10,812	8,634	25%
Tennessee	101,685	67,397	51%
Texas	400,968	287,092	40%
Utah	49,840	31,009	61%
Vermont	10,348	9,164	13%
Virginia	174,924	135,273	29%
Washington	118,083	99,840	18%
West Virginia	24,217	15,049	61%
Wisconsin	92,491	72,100	28%
Wyoming	7,766	7,576	3%
USA	5,453,064	4,100,000	33%

SOURCE: American Community Survey PUMS Data, 2012

		college-grad women, age 30–39	college-grad men, age 30–39	% more college-grad women than men, age 30–39
	MS	51,607	31,832	62%
	MO	129,125	98,101	32%
	MT	22,116	13,775	61%
	NE	46,017	39,295	17%
	NV	49,595	39,553	25%
	NH	32,015	25,530	25%
	NJ	268,940	212,678	26%
	NM	34,127	27,898	22%
	NY	572,111	455,788	26%
	NC	225,828	163,786	38%
	ND	17,242	13,787	25%
	OH	227,833	183,835	24%
	OK	66,272	52,920	25%
	OR	93,084	77,199	21%
	PA	295,475	229,360	29%
	RI	24,937	18,699	33%
	SC	94,389	69,742	35%
	SD	17,302	13,658	27%
	TN	136,006	103,818	31%
	TX	566,106	468,373	21%
	UT	66,551	73,226	-9%
	VT	13,461	9,400	43%
	VA	236,698	203,968	16%
	WA	168,399	146,065	15%
	WV	29,846	19,437	54%
	WI	127,204	98,668	29%
	WY	9,609	7,968	21%
	USA	7,362,748	5,983,763	23%

DATING MARKETS BY COUNTY

Even within the same state, sex ratios can vary significantly. In Texas, Harris County (home to Houston) has 52% more women than men among college grads age 22 to 29. But in Dallas County, the gender gap is only 23%.

COUNTY	college-grad women age 22–29	college-grad men age 22–29	
AK - Anchorage Municipality	4,765	2,018	
AL - Jefferson County (Birmingham)	13,704	11,583	
AZ - Maricopa County (Phoenix)	63,549	44,775	
AZ - Pima County (Tucson)	13,601	11,430	
CA - Alameda County (Oakland)	40,683	35,386	
CA - Contra Costa County (suburban San Francisco)	16,415	11,898	
CA - Fresno County	8,258	5,700	
CA - Los Angeles County	194,351	156,413	
CA - Marin County (suburban San Francisco)	2,793	2,378	
CA - Orange County (Anaheim, suburban LA)	63,463	48,640	
CA - Riverside County (suburban LA)	17,236	13,292	
CA - Sacramento County	21,533	18,265	
CA - San Bernardino County	22,150	14,424	
CA - San Diego County	64,026	58,202	
CA - San Francisco County	40,284	42,059	
CA - San Mateo County (suburban San Francisco)	14,610	12,095	
CA - Santa Clara County (San Jose)	40,889	45,736	

% more college-grad women than men, age 22–29	college-grad women age 30–39	college-grad men age 30–39	% more college-grad women than men, age 30–39
136%	7,066	5,320	33%
18%	17,780	16,378	9%
42%	89,162	79,069	13%
19%	18,339	15,437	19%
15%	62,754	57,984	8%
38%	27,734	26,708	4%
45%	10,787	10,176	6%
24%	250,565	221,684	13%
17%	8,048	7,149	13%
30%	85,531	80,153	7%
30%	34,112	27,692	23%
18%	30,967	25,110	23%
54%	33,918	24,596	38%
10%	92,542	81,670	13%
-4%	54,850	60,134	-9%
21%	27,566	24,974	10%
-11%	76,321	78,427	-3%

COUNTY	college-grad women age 22–29	college-grad men age 22–29	
CA - Sonoma County (suburban San Francisco)	4,296	3,566	
CO - Denver County	30,180	23,930	
CO - Douglas County*	5,624	4,482	
CT - Hartford County	18,939	14,240	
FL - Broward County (Fort Lauderdale)	28,728	16,791	
FL - Hillsborough County (Tampa Bay)	24,102	16,770	
FL - Miami-Dade County	41,341	32,511	
FL - Orange County (Orlando)	24,942	21,490	
FL - Palm Beach County (West Palm Beach)	17,007	14,841	
GA - Bibb County (Macon)	2,000	1,775	
GA - Fulton County**	30,464	27,456	
GA - Gwinnett County (suburban Atlanta)	11,741	7,287	
GA - Muscogee County (Columbus)	3,121	1,890	
HI - Honolulu County	20,909	11,064	
IA - Linn County (Cedar Rapids)	5,718	3,899	
IA - Polk County (Des Moines)	13,152	10,776	
IA - Scott County (Davenport)	4,662	2,192	
IL - Cook County (Chicago)	157,647	112,587	
IL - Lake County (suburban Chicago)	11,497	9,606	
LA - East Baton Rouge Parish	13,481	9,522	
LA - Orleans Parish (New Orleans)	11,687	8,052	
MA - Suffolk County (Boston)	45,132	35,095	
MD - Montgomery County (suburban DC)	28,731	22,465	

% more college-grad women than men, age 22–29	college-grad women age 30–39	college-grad men age 30–39	% more college-grad women than men, age 30–39
20%	8,835	6,641	33%
26%	30,938	29,352	5%
25%	14,365	12,996	11%
33%	22,855	21,136	8%
71%	43,618	36,303	20%
44%	32,988	25,614	29%
27%	61,133	51,063	20%
16%	30,669	27,852	10%
15%	25,538	22,459	14%
13%	2,114	1,975	7%
11%	43,737	37,704	16%
61%	24,057	18,370	31%
65%	2,769	3,543	-22%
89%	28,730	21,514	34%
47%	5,159	5,136	0%
22%	16,430	12,625	30%
113%	4,402	4,024	9%
40%	176,909	146,132	21%
20%	18,975	14,257	33%
42%	9,629	9,749	-1%
45%	10,422	8,963	16%
29%	29,381	27,780	6%
28%	43,538	38,677	13%

COUNTY	college-grad women age 22–29	college-grad men age 22–29	
MI - Oakland County (suburban Detroit)	27,208	20,298	
MI - Wayne County (Detroit)	22,112	16,056	
MN - Hennepin County (Minneapolis)	42,588	29,814	
MO - St. Louis City	11,561	8,746	
MO - St. Louis County (suburban St. Louis)	23,295	15,573	
NC - Durham County	11,811	8,609	
NC - Mecklenburg County (Charlotte)	28,011	22,697	
NC - Wake County (Raleigh)	27,696	19,584	
NJ - Morris County (suburban NYC)	12,473	9,147	
NJ - Somerset County (suburban NYC)	7,125	6,170	
NM - Bernalillo County***	11,099	8,533	
NV - Clark County (Las Vegas)	22,837	15,906	
NY - Dutchess County (suburban NYC)	4,643	2,234	
NY - Nassau County (suburban NYC)	31,704	24,018	
NY/NYC - Bronx County	19,324	11,152	
NY/NYC - Kings County (Brooklyn)	77,841	60,834	
NY/NYC - New York County (Manhattan)	114,892	82,784	
NY/NYC - Queens County	57,622	45,469	
NY/NYC - Richmond County (Staten Island)	9,060	9,356	
NY - Suffolk County (suburban New York City)	28,021	22,075	
NY - Westchester County (White Plains)	19,108	16,864	
OH - Cuyahoga County (Cleveland)	24,715	18,645	
OH - Franklin County (Columbus)	35,251	32,878	
OR - Multnomah County (Portland)	22,987	14,694	

% more college-grad women than men, age 22–29	college-grad women age 30–39	college-grad men age 30–39	% more college-grad women than men, age 30–39
34%	39,583	33,502	18%
38%	29,584	23,046	28%
43%	45,878	38,225	20%
32%	9,210	8,113	14%
50%	29,773	24,917	19%
37%	14,061	9,104	54%
23%	40,342	32,400	25%
41%	42,562	35,952	18%
36%	17,860	14,212	26%
15%	14,306	11,923	20%
30%	13,393	12,404	8%
44%	37,947	30,104	26%
108%	7,643	4,784	60%
32%	41,893	31,318	34%
73%	24,564	14,274	72%
28%	89,033	78,214	14%
39%	106,103	93,120	14%
27%	69,327	60,887	14%
-3%	13,068	7,556	73%
27%	41,350	28,051	47%
13%	30,182	25,406	19%
33%	29,919	24,715	21%
7%	37,439	31,971	17%
56%	35,857	28,689	25%

COUNTY	college-grad women age 22–29	college-grad men age 22–29	
OR - Washington County (suburban Portland)	13,952	10,716	
PA - Allegheny County (Pittsburgh)	42,378	31,684	
PA - Philadelphia County	47,121	35,364	
RI - Providence County	12,905	8,052	
TN - Shelby County (Memphis)	14,638	10,029	
TX - Bexar County (San Antonio)	24,884	21,589	
TX - Dallas County	45,404	36,906	
TX - Fort Bend County (suburban Houston)	10,383	6,930	
TX - Harris County (Houston)	85,091	55,817	
TX - Tarrant County (Ft. Worth)	29,000	20,686	
TX - Travis County (Austin)	38,420	30,371	
UT - Salt Lake County (Salt Lake City)	19,399	14,337	
UT - Utah County (Provo)	14,458	7,482	
VA - Fairfax County (suburban D.C.)	37,410	30,189	
WA - King County (Seattle)	60,327	53,636	
WA - Pierce County (suburban Seattle)	12,701	8,434	
Washington, D.C.	41,975	31,315	
WI - Milwaukee County	20,805	17,513	

* (and 49,000 of Jefferson and Elbert counties)
** (also 27,000 of DeKalb County)
*** (excludes 24,000 in Valencia County)
SOURCE: American Community Survey PUMS Data, 2012

% more college-grad women than men, age 22–29	college-grad women age 30–39	college-grad men age 30–39	% more college-grad women than men, age 30–39
30%	20,327	16,602	22%
34%	40,759	34,752	17%
33%	39,925	31,485	27%
60%	14,341	10,397	38%
46%	21,529	17,536	23%
15%	41,262	30,499	35%
23%	55,872	49,289	13%
50%	23,146	17,857	30%
52%	99,586	89,848	11%
40%	44,867	34,440	30%
27%	44,684	46,504	-4%
35%	28,442	29,730	-4%
93%	14,156	17,171	-18%
24%	53,530	52,495	2%
12%	80,455	81,615	-1%
51%	15,099	11,856	27%
34%	35,049	35,226	-1%
19%	25,529	20,682	23%

DEGREES AWARDED BY GENDER

American women caught up to men in higher education in the 1980s—and then never looked back.

BACHELORS

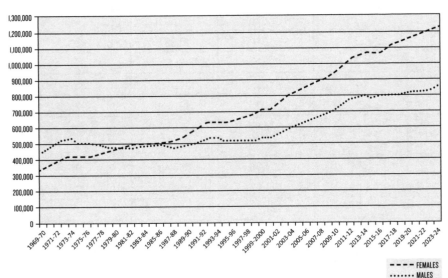

MASTERS

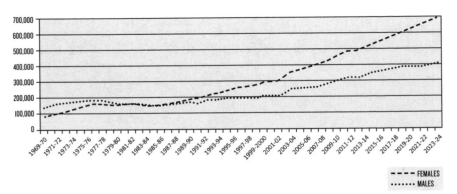

SOURCE: National Center for Education Studies (NCES)

HIGHER EDUCATION BY COUNTRY AND SEX

Even in China—a country with one-fifth more young men than young women overall—women still outnumber men in higher education.

COUNTRY	% more women than men in higher ed	COUNTRY	% more women than men in higher ed
Algeria	45%	Israel	32%
Argentina	56%	Italy	43%
Australia	38%	Japan	-10%
Austria	19%	Jordan	15%
Belgium	26%	Malaysia	20%
Canada *	29%	Mexico	-4%
Chile	10%	Netherlands	11%
China	11%	New Zealand	45%
Colombia	10%	Norway	58%
Croatia	40%	Pakistan	-8%
Cuba	64%	Poland	55%
Czech Republic	42%	Russian Federation	32%
Denmark	43%	Saudi Arabia	12%
Finland	23%	Spain	23%
France	25%	Sweden	51%
Germany	7%	Switzerland	-1%
Greece	3%	Thailand	27%
Hungary	32%	Turkey	-16%
Iceland	70%	United Kingdom	36%
India	-22%	United States	39%
Indonesia	-15%		
Ireland	4%		

SOURCES: World Bank

*Statistics Canada, CANSIM

BIBLIOGRAPHY

Adshade, Marina. *Dollars and Sex: How Economics Influences Sex and Love.* San Francisco: Chronicle Books, 2013.

Anokhin, Andrey P., Werner Lutzenberger, Andrey Nikolaev, and Niels Birbaumer. "Complexity of Electrocortical Dynamics in Children: Developmental Aspects." *Developmental Psychobiology* 36, no. 1 (2000): 9–22.

Barber, Nigel. "On the Relationship between Marital Opportunity and Teen Pregnancy: The Sex Ratio Question." *Journal of Cross-Cultural Psychology* 32, no. 3 (2001): 259–67.

———. "The Sex Ratio as a Predictor of Cross-National Variation in Violent Crime." *Cross-Cultural Research* 34, no. 3 (2000): 264–82.

Bedard, Kelly, and Elizabeth Dhuey. "The Persistence of Early Childhood Maturity: International Evidence of Long-Run Age Effects." *Quarterly Journal of Economics* 121, no. 4 (2006): 1437–472.

Cialdini, Robert B. *Influence: The Psychology of Persuasion.* Rev. Ed. New York: HarperCollins, 2007.

Clark, Dayna. "Ask A Mormon: There's a Mormons-Only Spring Break?" *GQ*, June 7, 2012, gq.com/news-politics/blogs/death-race/2012/06/ask-a-mormon-mormons-only-spring-break.html.

Crosser, Sandra. "Summer Birth Date Children: Kindergarten Entrance Age and Academic Achievement." *Journal of Educational Research* 84, no. 3 (1991): 140–146.

Durante, Kristina M., Vladas Griskevicius, Jeffry A. Simpson, Stephanie M. Cantú, and Joshua M. Tybur. "Sex Ratio and Women's Career Choice: Does a Scarcity of Men Lead Women to Choose Briefcase over Baby?" *Journal of Personality and Social Psychology* 103, no. 1 (2012): 121–34.

Early, David E., "Dating Service Schemes to Link All the Single Ladies of New York with Bay Area's Single Men." *San Jose Mercury News*, March 7, 2014.

Fein, Ellen, and Sherrie Schneider. *The Rules: Time-tested Secrets for Capturing the Heart of Mr. Right.* New York: Warner Books, 1995.

"Gender and Education: The Evidence on Pupils in England." Department for Education and Skills, The National Archives, webarchive.national archives.gov.uk/20130401151715/http://www.education.gov.uk/publications/eOrderingDownload/00389-2007BKT-EN.pdf.

Gimein, Mark. "The Eligible-Bachelor Paradox." Slate.com, April 9, 2008, slate.com/articles/arts/everyday_economics/2008/04/the_eligiblebachelor_paradox.html.

Goldin, Claudia, Lawrence F. Katz, and Ilyana Kuziemko. "The Homecoming of American College Women: The Reversal of the College Gender Gap." Cambridge, MA: National Bureau of Economic Research, 2006.

Griskevicius, Vladas, Joshua M. Tybur, Joshua M. Ackerman, Andrew W. Delton, Theresa E. Robertson, and Andrew E. White. "The Financial Consequences of Too Many Men: Sex Ratio Effects on Saving, Borrowing, and Spending." *Journal of Personality and Social Psychology* 102 (2012): 69–80.

Gross, Mart. "The Evolution of Parental Care." *Quarterly Review of Biology* 80, no. 1 (2005): 37–45.

Guttentag, Marcia, and Paul F. Secord. *Too Many Women?: The Sex Ratio Question.* Beverly Hills, CA: Sage Publications, 1983.

Halberstam, Yitta. "Purim and the Tyranny of Beauty: A Plea to Mothers of Girls in Shidduchim." *The Jewish Press*, March 19, 2012, jewishpress.com/sections/family/purim-and-the-tyranny-of-beauty-a-plea-to-mothers-of-girls-in-shidduchim/2012/03/19/0.

Holt, Lester. "Men Falling Behind Women." NBC News, March 5, 2011, nbcnews.com/id/41928806/ns/business-us_business/t/men-falling-behind-women.

Howard, Adam. "Affirmative Action for Men, Part Deux." *The Nation*, March 24, 2006, thenation.com/blog/affirmative-action-men-part-deux#.

Jacob, Brian A. "Where the Boys Aren't: Non-cognitive Skills, Returns to School and the Gender Gap in Higher Education." *Economics of Education Review* 21 (2002): 589–98.

"The Jewish Community Study of New York: 2011." ujafedny.org/who-we-are/our-mission/jewish-community-study-of-new-york-2011.

Kaleem, Jaweed. "Mormon Singles, LDS Singles Wards Rise as Members Delay Marriage." *Huffington Post*, September 14, 2012, huffingtonpost.com/2012/09/14/mormon-singles-lds-singles-wards-marriage_n_1875524.html.

Kennedy, Kelli. "Eating Disorders a Problem Among Orthodox Jews." Associated Press, December 10, 2010.

Kent, Margaret. *How to Marry the Man of Your Choice.* New York: Warner Books, 1987.

Kim, John S. "The Influence of Local Sex Ratio on Romantic Relationship Maintenance Processes." University of Minnesota Digital Conservancy, 2013, purl.umn.edu/158564.

Kring, Brunhild. "Generation Text Goes to College: A Developmental Perspective." *GROUP: Journal of the Eastern Group Psychotherapy Society* 36, no. 3 (2012): 233–42.

Lapp, Amber. "The Story We Tell About Love." *Family Studies*, July 21, 2014, family-studies.org/the-story-we-tell-about-love.

Lapp, David. "Stop Blaming Working-Class Men." *Family Studies*, April 25, 2014, family-studies.org/stop-blaming-working-class-men.

"Letters to the Editor." *The 5 Towns Jewish Times*, January 8, 2010, flipdocs .com/showbook.aspx?ID=10001763_629695.

Lovejoy, Ben. "Former Apple Managers Talk of the 24/7 Work Culture: These People Are Nuts." 9to5Mac, October 1, 2014. 9to5mac.com/2014/ 10/01/former-apple-managers-talk-of-the-247-work-culture-these-people-are-nuts.

Malkiel, Burton Gordon. *A Random Walk Down Wall Street.* New York: Norton, 1973.

"The Marriage Crunch." *Newsweek*, June 2, 1986.

Martinez, G., C. E. Copen, and J. C. Abma. "Teenagers in the United States: Sexual Activity, Contraceptive Use, and Childbearing, 2006–2010 National Survey of Family Growth." Atlanta, GA: National Center for Health Statistics, 2011.

"Matchmaker, Matchmaker, Am I Too Fat?" *The 5 Towns Jewish Times*, October 8, 2010, flipdocs.com/showbook.aspx?ID=10001763_193731.

Medved, Michael. "Hollywood's Three Big Lies." *Catholic Education*, May 1996, catholiceducation.org/articles/arts/al0033.html.

Molloy, John T. *Why Men Marry Some Women and Not Others: The Fascinating Research That Can Land You the Husband of Your Dreams.* New York: Warner Books, 2003.

"More Diagnoses of Hyperactivity in New C.D.C. Data." *The New York Times*, April 1, 2013.

Neff, B. D., and T. E. Pitcher. "Mate Choice for Non-additive Genetic Benefits: A Resolution to the Lek Paradox." *Journal of Theoretical Biology* 254 (2008): 147–55.

"Not Too Late to Meet Prince Charming After All." ABC News, May 26, 2006, abcnews.go.com/GMA/story?id=2007889.

Notkin, Melanie. *Otherhood: Modern Women Finding a New Kind of Happiness.* Berkeley, CA: Seal Press, 2014.

O'Brien, Robert M. "Sex Ratios and Rape Rates: A Power-Control Theory." *Criminology* 29, no. 1 (1991): 99–114.

Phillips, Rick, and Ryan T. Cragun. "Mormons in the United States 1990–2008: Socio-demographic Trends and Regional Differences." Hartford, CT: Trinity College, 2011.

Pierson, David. "China's Housing Boom Spells Trouble for Boyfriends." *Los Angeles Times*, June 21, 2010, articles.latimes.com/2010/jun/21/business/la-fi-china-bachelor-20100621.

Pollet, Thomas V., and Daniel Nettle. "Driving a Hard Bargain: Sex Ratio and Male Marriage Success in a Historical US Population." *Biology Letters* (2008): 31–33.

"The Real Reason You're Wanted in Silicon Valley/SF." BUZZ in the HUB, December 16, 2009, blog.bos.talentgraphz.com/2009/12/real-reason-you-wanted-in-silicon.html.

Regnerus, Mark, and Jeremy Uecker. *Premarital Sex in America: How Young Americans Meet, Mate, and Think about Marrying.* Oxford, UK: Oxford University Press, 2011.

Rey, José-Manuel. "The Carol Syndrome," *Plus*, June 1, 2009, plus.maths.org/content/carol-syndrome.

Reynolds, J. D., M. A. Coldwell, and F. Cooke. "Sexual Selection and Spring Arrival Times of Red-necked and Wilson's Phalaropes." *Behavioral Ecology and Sociobiology* 18 (1986): 303–10.

Rhoads, Steven. "Hookup Culture: The High Costs of a Low 'Price' for Sex." *Society* 49 (2012): 515–519.

Rosenfeld, M. J., and R. J. Thomas. "Searching for a Mate: The Rise of the Internet as a Social Intermediary." *American Sociological Review* 77 no. 4 (2012): pp. 523–47.

Rosin, Hanna. *The End of Men: And the Rise of Women.* New York: Riverhead Books, 2012.

Ruiz, Rebecca. "America's Vainest Cities." *Forbes*, November 29, 2007, forbes.com/2007/11/29/plastic-health-surgery-forbeslife-cx_rr_1129health.html.

Salamon, Michael J. *The Shidduch Crisis: Causes and Cures.* Jerusalem: Urim Publications, 2008.

"Sarah Lawrence." *Elective Affinities*, themilkandhoneyway.tumblr.com/post/38973794554/sarah-lawrence.

Sax, Leonard. *Boys Adrift: The Five Factors Driving the Growing Epidemic of Unmotivated Boys and Underachieving Young Men.* New York: Basic Books, 2007.

Shell, G. Richard. *Bargaining for Advantage: Negotiation Strategies for Reasonable People.* New York: Viking, 1999.

"The Shidduch Crisis Simply, and a Solution." *Ami Magazine*, January 16, 2013.

Sommers, Christina Hoff. *The War Against Boys: How Misguided Feminism Is Harming Our Young Men.* New York: Simon & Schuster, 2000.

South, Scott, and Katherine Trent. "Sex Ratios and Women's Roles: A Cross-National Analysis." *American Journal of Sociology* 93, no. 5 (1998): 1096–1115.

Stack, Peggy Fletcher. "Distinct Mormon Wards Help Mid-Singles Stay True to a Family Faith." *Salt Lake Tribune*, October 7, 2013.

———. "Why Young LDS Men Are Pushing Back Marriage," *Salt Lake Tribune*, April 29, 2011.

Steinberg, L. "A Social Neuroscience Perspective on Adolescent Risk-taking." *Developmental Review* 28, no. 1 (2008): 78–106.

Swift, Mike. "Silicon Valley Has Many Boys' Towns, But There Are Girls' Towns, Too." *San Jose Mercury News*, February 11, 2009.

"Time Out New York Sex Survey." Time Out, July 8, 2014, timeout.com/newyork/sex-dating/time-out-new-york-sex-survey-the-results-are-in.

Uecker, Jeremy E., and Mark D. Regnerus. "BARE MARKET: Campus Sex Ratios, Romantic Relationships, and Sexual Behavior." *Sociological Quarterly* 51, no. 3 (2010): 408–35.

Walsh, Anthony. *Biology and Criminology: The Biosocial Synthesis.* New York: Routledge, 2009.

Watkins, Christopher D., Benedict C. Jones, Anthony C. Little, Lisa M. Debruine, and David R. Feinberg. "Cues to the Sex Ratio of the Local Population Influence Women's Preferences for Facial Symmetry." *Animal Behaviour* 83, no. 2 (2012): 545–53.

Wei, Shang-Jin, and Xiaobo Zhang. "Sex Ratios, Entrepreneurship, and Economic Growth in the People's Republic of China." Cambridge, MA: National Bureau of Economic Research, 2011.

Williams, Alex. "The End of Courtship?" *The New York Times*, January 11, 2013.

———. "The New Math on Campus." *New York Times*, February 5, 2010.

Zweig, Jason. "Is Your Brain Wired for Wealth?" CNN, September 27, 2002, money.cnn.com/2002/09/25/pf/investing/agenda_brain_short.

INDEX

ACKNOWLEDGMENTS

When I first signed a contract to write a dating book, many folks had the same reaction: What does Laura think about that?

I guess it is a little odd for a 45-year-old man who has been happily married for 20-plus years to write a book about dating. Yet my wife, Laura Grossfield Birger, was supportive from the start. Despite my own uncertainty about whether I had the patience for a project with such a long gestation period, Laura never doubted that the book would be a success. So I want to kick off my acknowledgments by thanking my lovely, brilliant, and usually understanding wife for her feedback and encouragement—and also for being the finest amateur copy-editor on the planet (at least when she's not kicking butt in the courtroom).

My agent, Mel Parker of Mel Parker Books, provided fantastic counsel and representation throughout. Mel, thank you.

My editors at Workman Publishing—Susan Bolotin and Maisie Tivnan—were true allies. Maisie was my primary editor, and her suggestions, enthusiasm, and skillful editing made this book better. Suzie Bolotin, Workman's publisher, assisted in countless ways, most notably pushing me to make the book's statistical arguments more accessible to non-stat-geek readers. Suzie didn't even grumble when one of her young, single, female assistants decided to abandon New York City (and thus Workman too) after reading my initial book proposal. Another tip of the hat goes to Workman's stellar marketing, publicity, and production team—specifically Noreen Herits, Jessica Wiener, Selina Meere, Amanda Hong, and Becky Terhune.

My friend and fellow journalist Hilary Macht Felgran read an early draft of the book and was a frequent sounding board. Other friends and colleagues who were generous with ideas, advice, feedback, and sources include: Wendy Blake, Monica Owusu Breen, Ylonda Gault Caviness, Lisa Takeuchi Cullen, Amy Feldman, Leigh Gallagher, Andrea Bennett Gardner, Katherine Reynolds Lewis, Falisha Mamdani, Ellen McGirt, Lysa Price, Catherine Pritchard, Nelson Schwartz, Patricia Sellers, Rabbi Jeffrey Sirkman, Stephanie Smith, Jacques Steinberg, and Amy Wolfcale.

The chapter on the marriage crises affecting Mormons and Orthodox Jews happens to be my personal favorite. Going in, I knew very little about either group, which meant I leaned on the assistance and sharp insights of several key sources—among them Ryan Cragun, Steve Rinehart, Hannah Wheelwright, Lisa Elefant, Michael Salamon, Rabbi Jonathan Morgenstern, and Rabbi Steven Weil. I'm also grateful to Jeff Bloom—the hedge fund manager who called me about a job but wound up tipping me off about the Shidduch Crisis.

Demographer Susan Weber-Stoger, a senior researcher in the Queens College sociology department, helped me drill down into national, state, and local Census data in ways I never could have done on my own. Thank you, Susan. I also want to thank Queens College sociology professor Andrew Beveridge, not only for connecting me with Susan but also for referring me to Gary Gates, the LGBTQ demographics expert at UCLA.

Hanna Rodriguez Farrar—today a college administrator in California and once upon a time my art history teaching assistant (and occasional squash partner) at Brown University— helped me brainstorm about many of the gender-ratio-related challenges facing American colleges and universities.

Jonathan Schor, the former editor-in-chief of *The California Tech*, the CalTech student newspaper, did me an enormous favor when he arranged the focus group with students on CalTech dating life.

One of my hopes is that this book gives the late Marcia

Guttentag the mainstream recognition she deserved but never received (at least outside of academia) for her pioneering research on human sex ratios. Guttentag's son Michael and her friends Susan Salasin and Lois-ellen Datta were extremely generous with their time and their memories. For that, I am truly grateful.

Good reporters are a product of good editors, and I'm fortunate to have learned from and worked with some phenomenal newspaper and magazine editors over my 25-year career. Among them: Greg David, Bob Safian, Hank Gilman, Glenn Coleman, the late (and greatly missed) Cynthia Rigg, Eric Gelman, Denise Martin, Steve Malanga, Tom Kearney, Eric Pooley, and Andy Serwer.

I want to thank photographer Sandra Wong Geroux for making me look so good in my author photo, and web designer Joel Myers for helping me build the Dateonomics .com and JonBirger.com websites.

Thank you to my parents Barbara and Jordan Birger, my brother Chet Birger, my friend Dave Carey, and my in-laws Toby and Bernie Grossfield for their love and encouragement. I also need to thank my sons, Alex, Zach, and Eli, for putting up with the sex-ratio talk that always seemed to erupt in the stands of their school concerts and their Little League games. Having your dad write a dating book can be a little embarrassing, but my boys handled it with grace and good humor. Alex and Zach, my teenage twins, were also a never-ending source of funny title ideas—from "Man-ball" to "50 Shades of Freakonomics."

Finally, I want to thank the pseudonymous men and women who entrusted me with their personal stories about sex and dating in today's lopsided dating markets. Not all their interviews made it into the book, but every one of them influenced it.